3.95
wh

D1012537

WINNING ISN'T ALWAYS 1ST PLACE

DALLAS GROTEN

BETHANY HOUSE PUBLISHERS
MINNEAPOLIS, MINNESOTA 55438
A Division of Bethany Fellowship, Inc.

Photos by Dick Easterday

Scripture quotations are taken from the King James Version of the Bible, and from the Revised Standard Version of the Bible, copyright 1946, 1952 © 1971, 1973. Used by permission.

Copyright © 1983
Dallas Groten
All Rights Reserved

Published by Bethany House Publishers
A Division of Bethany Fellowship, Inc.
6820 Auto Club Road, Minneapolis, MN 55438

Printed in the United States of America

Library of Congress Cataloging in Publication Data

Groten, Dallas, 1951-
    Winning isn't always first place

    Summary: A collection of thirty-seven devotions based on actual competitions, triumphs, and defeats of the Wykoff, Minnesota, track team.
    1. Youth—Prayer-books and devotions—English.
[1. Prayer books and devotions.   2. Winning and losing]
I. Title.
BV4850.G76   1983   248.4'841'03   83-14930
ISBN 0-87123-613-3 (pbk.)

Winning Isn't Always First Place

"Far better it is to dare mighty things, to win glorious triumphs, even though checkered by failure, than to take rank with those poor spirits who neither enjoy much nor suffer much, because they live in the gray twilight that knows not victory or defeat."

Theodore Roosevelt

Dedication

To Caroline, who *always* believed
in me

The Author

DALLAS GROTEN holds a B.A. in sociology from Augsburg College in Minneapolis. He was head track coach and counselor at Wykoff High School in Wykoff, Minnesota. Dallas is married and presently enrolled at Faith Evangelical Lutheran Seminary in Tacoma, Washington.

Acknowledgments

I would like to thank the young men and women of the track team whom I coached at Wykoff High School. These people are the true champions of this book. A special word of thanks goes out to the following heroes and heroines: Jon, Paul, Mary, and Rodel Eberle; Mark Eickhoff; Dan Evers; Charlene, Dan, and Mike Hellerud; Jeff Kappers; Phil Kaun; Dan and Scott Kellogg; Brenda and Mitch Lentz; Charles McPherson; Doug Meyer; Larry Mulhern; Curt Nash; Maureen O'Byrne; Donnie Ramaker; Brenda Rollie; Dave Root; Patti Sanford; Darvin Schmidt; Brian Schwier; Eric and Ken Shipton; Michelle Sikkink; Brenda Vreeman; Sadie Winslow; Steve Winter; and Jeanne Wolfgram.

Contents

Introduction

With one glance at the team I knew that everything battled against us.

Wykoff is a tiny town of 450 possessing a small school district. I could bribe the entire senior class into coming out for track and still have a small team. And this season my miniature track team would wrestle with several big schools during its grueling schedule. In this sport, the larger team usually has the advantage over the smaller team. My team would have to confront many obstacles this year.

The first obstacle was our clay and mud track. If nature did not turn it into a brown ooze, the kids would be able to run on it. But to ask for a spring without rain was too much; we were, for all practical purposes, a team without a track. The second obstacle was Wykoff's ruralness. Spring is planting time and track is a spring sport. And farming was the main source of income for most of my team members' families. Parental demands that my athletes help out in the fields would conflict with practices and meets.

There was no need for me to number all the obstacles; the list seemed endless: prom, the senior class trip, graduation, etc.

But perhaps the biggest obstacle of all would be the coach. I was the only coach of the entire track program, comprising junior and senior high boys and girls—a total of fifty students. Not only would I have to supervise workouts for high jumpers, pole vaulters, shot putters, discus throwers, sprinters, hurdlers, and distance runners, I would also have to teach basics to the beginners, sharpen the skills of the experienced, provide leadership and discipline, and nurse injuries. How could one man ever do all that? Me—especially.

To top it all off, Wykoff's athletic teams, due to their school's small size, had developed an inferiority complex. I now envisioned many a long, silent bus ride home after each defeat at a track meet. I wasn't sure I wanted to inflict such agony on the young people who sat before me on the gym floor.

"Could I have your attention?" I said.

When one gathers young men and women together, there is always giggling, flirting, and showing off. But on this day there was little of such behavior. My team appeared ready to listen.

"We face many obstacles," I said. "But winning isn't always first place; it isn't always bringing home trophies or medals. You may gain first place in the shot put, only to go home and find out that your father had just died. Your relay team may snatch a first place at the regional, but you may flunk an English test the next day because your concentration was on the race rather than on school."

Some of them were swaying in their seats. A few were even starting to whisper to one another. *Perhaps they don't want to listen to me after all*, I thought. *Maybe I'm wasting my time . . .*

"Losing seems to be just as much a part of life as winning," I continued. "You cannot live without experiencing some type of loss at some time."

I looked into their faces. Some of them appeared skeptical. Their respect was not going to be handed to me. I would have to earn it. But I also noticed that many faces seemed to ache with a profound thirst; and those faces drank in each of my words.

"We can't be afraid of defeat," I said. "We have to go forward with courage and do our best. We have to develop the will to win while we learn to live with our defeats. But what is most important, we have to see that losing is often winning in disguise. We have to understand the victory of defeat."

Now every eye was strong upon me. But those eyes were puzzled. *This is it*, I thought. *They must understand what I'm about to say, or there will be no team.*

"It would be more of a victory for our team to *go* to state and take last place than it would be for another team to *win* state. It would be more of a victory for a girl, who can't make our team, to become valedictorian than for a guy to win the 'Most Valuable Player' trophy and then drop out of school. It would be more of a victory for a young man, tormented by his teammates because of homeliness, old clothes, or the color of his skin, to even stay on the team than it would be for another to earn a letter. And it would be more of a victory for one suffering self-doubts to come in last place in a race, facing the humiliation with dignity, than it would be for a self-assured jock to break the tape."

Again I examined my team's faces. Yes, they were all listening, but did they really understand?

"I hope you learn something important about being a human being this season. Track is a learning experience. In fact, did you know that the Bible talks about track and field? First Corinthians 9 is filled with track analogies. In life, you may find yourself using track phrases such as 'winning the race' or 'conquering the next hurdle' or 'leaping to new achievements.' This is because the virtues needed for success in track are the same virtues needed for success in life: hard work, dedication, sacrifice, perseverance, and team work."

There was no more giggling or flirting. In fact, the locker room was silent. Whether that silence would transform itself into tears of defeat or shouts of victory would be revealed in the weeks ahead.

Have you known loss in your life? Have you been wounded by the sting of defeat? Have you been called a failure? If you have, my prayer is that this book can help you. For *Winning Isn't Always First Place* is not about track and field; it's about turning losses into wins—and finding victory in every defeat. This book shows how "all things work together for good to them that love God" (Rom. 8:28, KJV); it shows what it means to follow Jesus Christ. In this book, track and field is the stage on which this search for the victory in every defeat is carried out.

However, this book does not tell about Olympians or superstars. It tells about ordinary young men and women. These devotionals are parables based on hard truth. The actual triumphs of Wykoff's track team are recorded in each chapter.

However, so as not to exploit or hurt the good people of Wykoff, and in order to tell the truth with love, I must state that the characters in this book—though portraying real ideas, feelings, and situations—are fictitious. Each character is a composite of several real people, courageous spirits that were a part of Wykoff track or of my twelve years of experience with youth work.

The heroes and champions of this volume are the very real people who enacted the incidents I have written about. I write with intimacy because the defeats of each young man and woman are my defeats as well.

"But thanks be to God, who gives us the victory through our Lord Jesus Christ" (1 Cor. 15:57, RSV).

1

It's Failure Only If You Stay in the Dirt

Sam was the first athlete in the history of Wykoff to compete in a state tournament. The sport would be track, and his event high hurdles. The meet was only a week away.

He had been hurdling for only a year. He and I, his coach, were very excited. Now Sam would need a good track to practice on, a track better than our primitive clay and mud affair. I asked the coach of a neighboring town, Spring Valley, if Sam could train on his track. He approved. Although Spring Valley's cinder track was not the best, it was far better than our own.

It was our first practice at the Spring Valley track. The sky was darkened with storm clouds; the air smelled of approaching rain.

I set up three hurdles. We were going to work on proper hurdle form before any attempt at practicing a full line of ten hurdles.

I talked to Sam for a few moments. I assured him that he was going to be the state champion. He eyed me through his thick glasses and smiled his slow, lazy smile. Joy and anticipation lit his face.

Sam wanted to achieve a great deal in life. And he knew that in order to attain his goals, he would have to dream, toil, believe, and never give up. He listened carefully to his teachers and coaches, hoping that what he learned from them would help him fulfill his dreams. Sam was an "A" student and a member of the band, choir, and the National Honor Society; he was the captain of both the basketball and track team. He intended to pursue a career in the Air Force.

And yes, he was the first person in his small town to enter state competition in *any* sport. All of Wykoff was proud of him. And the whole town projected its hope and desire for victory toward Sam. For the next week, he would be Wykoff.

Sam poised himself in the starting blocks. He gritted his teeth with a determination that I had never seen on an athlete his age. He wanted victory. He knew that every step he took in practice would be vitally important. To him, practicing for the state tournament was the start of a brand new season.

As drops of rain began to pelt us, I called out the starter's cadence. "Runners to your mark!"

Sam flexed the muscles in his legs. *Think state. State. Victory.*

"Set!"

He arched his fingers and leaned forward, putting all his weight upon his fingertips. *Grit. Proper hurdle form is what's important now,* he thought. *Work on form. Work on speed. Work on grit. Work and win state . . .*

"Go!"

He exploded out of the blocks. He ran a full-force sprint to the first hurdle. Over. His lead leg was out, his opposite arm down and forward; he was leaning with his trunk. He could have balanced a glass of water on top of his head—perfect form. I thrilled as I watched the making of a true champion.

He sprinted for the next hurdle.

"Pump your arms!" I yelled.

He pumped his arms like a powerful machine and vaulted over the second hurdle.

Sprint. Third hurdle. Lead leg. Opposite arm. Lean with the trunk.

But his trail leg was too high. His toe caught the top of the hurdle. He fell.

Pain. Kaleidoscopic colors. Pain. Gray sky. Cindered earth. Pain. Pouring rain. Face of coach. Torn flesh. Pain.

Sam rolled upon the track, but soon jerked to his feet. He was bent over in agony. I could see the bruised knees and thighs, the blood oozing from the cuts. The rain was gaining momentum, adding to our misery.

Sam had never let the hurdles scare him. That had been his strong point as an athlete. But it was raining hard, and I knew that I would have to take him indoors to clean those cuts. Yet, I also knew there was one thing I would have to do first.

"Sam."

He looked up at me, adjusting his glasses.

"Run them again."

Silence. The falling rain.

Again he looked down at his bleeding legs. He thought of his fall at the third hurdle. Going back to the blocks and running the whole thing a second time did not appeal to him at all. He didn't even want to look at a hurdle. But there was state—and his goals.

"I said, run them again."

Reluctantly he nodded his head. And in pain he trotted back to the starting blocks. The white needles of rain made Sam get into position quickly.

"Runners to your mark!" I called, the rain dripping from my hair. "Set!"

Sam gritted his teeth, every muscle tensed to dive out of those blocks. The pain showed. But there was something different on his face this time: fear.

"Go!"

His feet dug into the wet cinders. Step. Step. Step.

First hurdle. Lead leg. Opposite arm. The lean with the trunk, perfect.

Step. Step. Step. Second hurdle. Perfect.

Step. Step.

Grit your teeth, Sam. Believe it. Believe you can do it. Be brave. State.

Step.

Third hurdle, perfect.

The sky erupted with thunder and pouring rain.

I patted Sam on the back and together we ran for shelter, to clean his wounds.

Your Turn

The longer you lie in the blood of your own failure, the worse off you will be. The longer you shelter yourself from a confrontation with the sin in your life, the greater your fear of that sin will grow.

If you sin, confront it immediately. Tell God that you are sorry, ask Him to forgive you because of Jesus. Leave sin buried in the mud and the blood behind you. Then run through life with a new determination. If you should trip, Christ is always there to pick you up in mercy.

"If we confess our sins, he is faithful and just to forgive us our sins, and to cleanse us from all unrighteousness" (1 John 1:9, KJV).

1. Is guilt troubling you? Is there a sin in your life that you have not confessed to God?
2. Do you hurdle over the troubles set before you by depending on Christ? Or do you knock these troubles over and therefore hurt yourself because you face them with your own strength?
3. Think of the last time that you tripped and fell in your walk with Christ. What positive lessons did you learn from that failure?
4. Are you forging into the future? Or are you wallowing in self-pity about your own cuts and bruises?
5. Think of all the "hurdles" or obstacles that you repeatedly stumble over in your life. Can you recognize some pattern in your stumbling that can be avoided?
6. What one thing will you do tomorrow to avoid falling in your Christian walk?

2

The Only *Thing*

"Winning isn't everything; it's the only thing," said Vince Lombardi,* who coached the Green Bay Packers to win five National Football League Championships. Now, I'm not out to tear down a great American hero like Vince Lombardi. He had many admirable qualities. But I would like to take a closer look at the phrase "Winning isn't everything; it's the only thing" and show how that phrase has been misused.

The first year that I coached track and field, my team had a Friday night invitational, under the lights, at Spring Valley. I was living in Spring Valley and many people that I knew there would be at the track meet. Track fans from both Wykoff and the Valley would be judging my ability as a coach on this night, and my athletes were considered the underdogs.

As the evening progressed, my team was doing quite well, getting firsts in several events.

Then Rick told me he couldn't run the 800-meter leg in the sprint medley relay. Rick was also our pole vaulter and he had been having leg problems all season. He told me that running the 800 at this meet might ruin his twelve-and-a-half-foot vaulting at the big conference meet coming up.

Tonight I needed his speed in the 800-meter leg of the relay. Without him, we'd lose the race—and the meet. But Rick couldn't run. I trusted his experience and his judgment. I knew he wasn't lying; his legs needed rest. But I had a cold, fearful ache in my gut. The crowd was expecting great things from our team.

---

*Some sources claim Lombardi actually said, "Winning isn't everything, but wanting to is."

Panicky, I could envision an article in the *Spring Valley Tribune* wallowing in the fact that Spring Valley had beat the Wykoff hicks. I thought of my neighbors asking me the next morning how the meet had gone. I thought about entering the bus after the meet, and facing my defeated team. I thought of three strong sprinters eager to win the relay.

But most of all I faced the fact that I was about to become a losing coach. *I* would be a *loser*.

We have to get some points in the sprint medley, I thought. *We have to win this meet.*

"Ted!" I yelled.

Ted was talking to three teammates, his back toward me. He looked around; I motioned, and he walked in my direction.

"What is it, Coach?"

"I want you to run the 800-leg in the sprint medley."

"*Me?*"

I nodded.

"But I'm a sprinter and a weightman. I'm used to throwing shot and discus. Look at my build. Do I look like a half-miler?"

"You're the only man I can spare. You're running it."

Ted gave me several good arguments as to why he shouldn't be running, all of them valid and true.

"I am the coach," I replied. "It's just twice around the track." I was thinking *win,* win at any cost.

Ted started to stretch, preparing himself for the race. He thought I had picked him to run the 800 as a way of demonstrating that our team had to confront every obstacle bravely and not give up. Even though Rick could not run, we would do our best, despite weakness, and therefore show the opponents and our community the qualities of determination, sacrifice, and courage. Ted accepted all this. A champion is first a champion in attitude. His motives were great. If only he knew mine . . .

The gun!

Our first runner took off with the baton. 200 meters of precision and speed. He handed off to the second 200-meter man. Nothing but aggressive determination. The 400-meter man grabbed the baton and sprinted the grueling leg with everything he had. Agony clawed at him as he handed off to Ted.

We were in good position, close to the lead. Ted started strong, inching his way to the head of the pack. Then, at the

200-meter mark, he slowed as if he had rammed into a wooden fence. He was dead tired—with 600 meters to go. The other runners soon passed him.

Ted was at least 150 meters behind as the next-to-last runner crossed the finish line. The starter was about to begin the next event when he noticed that Ted was still not in. The crowd watched in impatient, embarrassed silence as Ted limped across the finish line.

The medley team was angry with Ted. They had run as hard as they could, only to have Ted ruin their chance for even a single point.

I watched an exhausted and humiliated Ted stagger to the infield. Gasping, he fell on his knees and vomited. I walked over to him, to help him to his feet, to comfort him. Then I saw his tears. I realized what *I* had done.

I had let the spirit of "winning is the only thing" possess and control me. I had thus abused and humiliated another human being—and a fourteen-year-old boy at that. I had not made Ted run for any lofty or exalted reasons. I had forced Ted to carry the baton simply because I wanted to glorify *myself* by guiding my team to victory.

Somehow, as a Christian I had thought that I was above "winning is the only thing." But now I realized that I had been worshiping winning. I finally realized it when I saw the damage I had done to another human being.

Your Turn

Winning is a reward for hard work, courage, and determination. Winning is a worthy goal. But when you believe that "winning is the only thing," you are putting winning higher than God, on a plane where you bow to it and worship it. God is the only one worthy of first place in your life. Not sports, not riches, not fame, not victory. If you put anything or anyone else higher than God, no matter how virtuous your motives seem, you will end up hurting God, others, and especially yourself.

With no apology to Vince Lombardi, *God* is the only thing.

"I am the Lord thy God, which have brought thee out of the

land of Egypt, out of the house of bondage. Thou shalt have no other gods before me" (Ex. 20:2-3, KJV).

1. What is the most important thing in your life?
2. Is there anything in life that you want more than Christ?
3. Have you ever hurt a person because you put something else higher than God? Explain.
4. Think of the last time that you had a "victory" in your life. Have new problems developed because of that victory?
5. Have you ever come in last place in something? How did it make you feel?
6. In what ways can you put Christ first in your life today and tomorrow?

3

Pain

I was judging the baton exchanges in the girls' 400-meter relay. All the hand-offs were crisp. Each baton passed from the incoming runner to the out-going runner within the exchange zone. Then, I heard the *crack!*

Sherri gripped the baton as pain gripped her face. A bone had slashed out-of-joint close to her knee. Yet her body kept moving; she refused to stop running. Her powerful legs pumped and carried her spirit toward that blurred finish line, 100 meters away.

I knew of Sherri's worries about her legs, fearing that she would one day suffer from a bone problem. But I also understood her terror of letting down the team. She commanded the anchor position; she was always the last person to receive the baton, so the race depended upon her. Her relay team had been ahead when the baton was slapped into her hand. But now, one by one, in swift and merciless procession, the other girls were gaining on her.

I knew the pain that she battled both within and without. For I had heard the crack and now that crack echoed inside my brain. But Sherri muffled the agony. She was fighting a limp, or anything else that would distract her from the finish line. That sweet goal seemed so hazy to her in the distance, and was rocketing closer all the time. *But the pain!*

The other girls, batons tight in their hands, were pulling closer and closer. The crowd screamed. *Don't limp. Don't hobble. Run!* She leaned, and broke the tape. Sherri's relay team was victorious, and when her teammates saw her collapse at the finish line, her leg no longer able to hold her, she did not need to advertise anything. Her team swarmed around her—desperate to help.

I bounded toward her. There was Sherri curled on the ground, clutching her knee. I knew that she had sacrificed high jumping in the conference meet next week to cross that finish line today for the sake of her team. In track, as in so many areas, we win in one event, only to lose in another.

Sherri had struggled through the pain, not allowing it to keep her from reaching her goal. She did not want the pain to erupt into a shaking and wobbly body that would take her attention away from victory and the building up of her team. She did *not* flaunt or advertise her pain to the crowd. She knew that her job was to cross the finish line, and that's what she did. She crossed that line a champion.

Your Turn

All of us suffer, and we know that it is of great comfort and importance to have the healing attention of our brothers and sisters in Christ. But God does not want us wailing and crying to the world that the devil and pain are whipping us, controlling us, choking us. After all, *who* is your God? Pain or the Lord? Evil or the Christ?

God does not want us to exaggerate or advertise our trials. He doesn't want us to grumble our way to heaven. In the same manner, God does not want us to wear our pains and our trials upon our chests like ribbons and track medals. And He does not want us collapsing in His arms, exhausted, because we have refused to give a burden to Him to carry. Instead, God waits for us to give our pain to Him so that we may run freely in Christ.

"We must not . . . grumble, as some of them did and were destroyed by the Destroyer" (1 Cor. 10:9-10, RSV).

1. When you hear others grumble about their pain and their trials, what effect does this have on you?
2. Is there any pain now lashing at your life that you want to keep and not give to God?

3. Have you ever been angry at God because of a pain in your life?
4. Do you ever feel that you have to exaggerate or grumble about your pain to others? Why do you do this?
5. What is the difference between advertising your pain and telling your problems to another?
6. What time of the day tomorrow can you set aside to tell your problems to God, and a parent, or some trusted person?

4

Sometimes the Winners Are the Losers

I gripped the iron bar and pulled myself up to a standing position. And then, I ripped into the team.

"You can *do* it," I said. I knew they wanted to win. I too wanted them to win, not just a symbolic victory, but a real flesh-and-blood victory. However, their school was small, they lacked experience, and they were stuck with their "Spartan track," as the newspapers called it. All these negatives had built a roadblock between each young man and the possibility of believing that he could honestly be *victorious* in competition with the big schools.

"*You* can win. *Think win*," I said, my feet wobbling in the sway of the bus. Kenny, our jolly driver, smiled at me in the rearview mirror. I was the only person he allowed to stand while the bus was moving.

I looked into each face: Ted, Rick, Sam, Don, Goldie, Warren. Suddenly, it happened! Yes, at that moment I saw the dream ignite in their eyes. After many heartbreaking weeks, it had finally dawned on them that *this* team could really accomplish something glorious at this track meet. They knew that each one of them could be a *winner*. But it wasn't my words that had inspired them. Their practice combined with their own ambition had now, at this moment, been translated into confidence. That confidence in turn had uncovered the great will to win that was deep inside every member of the Wykoff community. How could I have doubted it? *This* team, "the smallest school around," wanted to win. My team *did* believe in itself.

"Do your best!" I called above the rumble of the bus. "Do

your best, and no matter how this track meet turns out, I'll be proud of you."

Our bus pulled into the opposing school's parking lot. And as I strained my eyes through the steamed glass of the window, I could see their track and practice field. But as suddenly as a dream had turned the heart of my team to fire, I was both overwhelmed and devastated.

Our opponents did not have the most sophisticated facility, but they did have *people*—coaches, assistant coaches, and more competitors. Coaches who could specialize in field events, or distance running or sprinting. The head coach wasn't required to cover every screaming need himself. Yes, our opponents had coaches, but what was more, they had more athletes.

The greater the number of men and women who come out for a track team, the greater the probability that that team has supreme athletes. The coach could have two quality athletes running the hurdles, or the 100-meter dash, instead of just one, like me. Athletes could specialize also; each one could concentrate on just one or two events and not exhaust himself.

My guys, on the other hand, had to be in four events at a track meet, just to fill every event. And many times they staggered to the last event, weary with pain and exhaustion. Sometimes I couldn't even scrape together a relay team for a certain event. But the opposing coach, with more people, always could, even if his relay team was composed of four seventh graders. And that brought out still another advantage our opponents had.

They could get points in a meet even through their poor athletes. Only my best athletes could conquer a first place in an event at a small meet like this. But a school with the numbers could reel in a fourth or a fifth place with poor athletes who simply ran, or even crawled, because our small school could supply only one or two runners for that event.

The gun for the 110 hurdles!

I watched with a strong sense of frustration. Sam was lagging behind everybody. But soon he was crashing his way forward. He passed one hurdler, then another, and yet another, still another. He fired across the line in second place, Sam's best time ever. Then the winner of that race, from the host school, asked his coach if he could go in and shower. The coach said yes. But Sam had to report to the high jump.

100-meter dash!

I saw Goldie straining, picking up speed, hitting his full potential at the 75-meter mark. He gritted his teeth, thinking "win." He pulled in a first place with one of his best times ever. But Goldie could not bathe in the glory: he had to prepare for the upcoming 400-meter run.

I watched Rick attack the pole vault with super courage. Don proved his mastery in both the shot and discus.

Gun shot!

Warren was my top miler, my only miler, and he always put out respectable times simply on the strength of his talent. My goal had been to combine that talent with hard work. I was confident that with such a mixture, our team would be blessed with an outstanding runner.

At the first lap Warren was grappling with the front of the pack. He was setting a pace I couldn't believe, pushing that first lap faster than I had ever seen him run.

"Warren!" I called. "If you're running first place, you've got to stay there. Stay there!"

He nodded at me. As he went into the second lap, he maintained the same speed. I wondered how his endurance was holding; perhaps he *could* hold onto his pace and keep it against such powerful milers. But would he be able to speed up and *beat* these runners?

"You're halfway, Warren!" I called. His teammates screamed from the sidelines, encouraging him on.

The first-place runner bolted faster, with the second man close behind. The fourth miler, who was immediately behind Warren, shot forward, as did the fifth man. Soon both milers passed Warren.

I could hear the screams from his teammates pounding in Warren's ears. I could see the pain in his face. I could see the strain in his muscles. I knew that dizziness, nausea, and exhaustion awaited him.

Then, abruptly, Warren blasted forward with an energy I didn't know he possessed, energy that he had somehow pulled out of a secret chamber deep within. His newfound speed caused the three in front of him to move even faster. They flew through the swift third lap.

Spikes speared the cinder underfoot. The runners fired ahead into a future that held only one first place.

"C'mon Warren! Go get 'em!" each one of his teammates yelled in fury. And in that fast lap, I saw Warren at the heels of fourth place, with "win" dancing wildly in his eyes. He dug in and shot for victory. He stretched his arms out in front of him and put all his strength into each brutal step.

It was then I realized that Warren believed the words I had hammered into him. He believed he could be a champion. This team no longer possessed an inferiority complex, and it never would again. Each member knew that he could win. And each person was at this track meet to *prove* that he could win.

Then, as Warren fought his way into the last lap, I made a startling discovery. It was mathematically impossible for Wykoff to win this meet.

It was true. Despite the broken records and the first places and Warren's magnificent performance and the fact that my team was competing as if the universe were at stake, Wykoff would not win this meet. The host team had *too many athletes*. Wykoff could not win if it had to play the numbers game.

The last lap. The early fast pace that Warren had set stabbed everyone with exhaustion. So the final lap was more like a heavy limp around the track. But fight was in Warren's face. He battled on despite iron legs, a parched throat, and wheezing lungs. Then, he muscled his way in front of the frightened young man before him. Warren finished third place, giving his team points, running his best personal time, and beating some excellent distance men in the process.

My voice was hoarse from shouting. But with my fresh revelation I no longer wanted to shout. I wanted to shield my team from my calculations. I didn't want them to know the truth.

We had done more than we thought possible. We had played fair. We had proved ourselves. But now, no matter what we did, it was mathematically impossible for us to win this meet.

But my team would know all this soon anyway. What would that knowledge do for the team? How would they react, knowing that if they excelled beyond their ability, they would still lose track meets?

Would my team die?

Cold reality slapped me hard in the face. I had told the team they could be winners. Was I lying to them? Was my dream of getting a trophy at the district track meet a fantasy?

"What's the matter, Coach?" Warren asked, trying to catch his breath.

"Oh, nothing, nothing." I brushed it off and put my arm around him. "Great race, Warren. You were fantastic."

"Thanks," he gasped again. "What's the matter?"

I didn't know what to say.

"We're going to lose, aren't we?"

"Warren," I stammered. ". . . You know?"

"We're too small a team. But you wait until we get to regions. Up there, things are evened out more."

"But you ran your heart out," I protested. "Everybody did. Everybody did great! I saw courage and drive and skill all over the place today. You guys broke records. But the statistics in the *Rochester Post Bulletin* won't say that. The statistics will just call us losers . . ."

Warren bent over and coughed; his breath was slowly coming back. "Maybe sometimes the winners are really the losers," he said. "Maybe the newspapers don't know that. But each guy on this team does."

Then, he placed his hand on my shoulder. "It's okay, Coach," he said.

Your Turn

Long ago people thought they were doing humanity a favor by nailing a "madman" to a cross. He claimed to be the Son of God.

When they killed Jesus, these killers called themselves "victors," winning favor in the eyes of the world. These same people called Jesus a "loser." He was expected to conquer the Romans and wear a golden crown. Instead, He died as a criminal between two thieves.

But the loser turned out to be the victor, gaining salvation and eternal life for all who would believe and follow Him. And the "victors" were really the losers, trapped into eternity knowing they had murdered the Son of God.

"For what is a man profited, if he shall gain the whole world and lose his own soul?" (Matt. 16:26, KJV).

1. Did you ever win something by cheating? How did you feel afterward?
2. Maybe sometimes the winners are really the losers. Can you think of any people to whom such a phrase could apply?
3. Read the Bible passage on page 33 again. What does it mean to you?
4. Have you ever been involved in a cause that seemed "mathematically impossible" to win?
5. What positive benefits can a person gain from a "lost cause"?
6. What can you do tomorrow to be a victor in the eyes of God?

5

Winners Don't Know How to Quit

Marcy had guts; that's what made her an excellent half-miler. Now she was at the district track meet. But our athletic district was outstanding, in one of the best high school track regions in Minnesota.

The gun.

The runners were a massive pack, staying in their own lanes until they got the flag at the first turn.

Marcy was out front, running in her own style, a style that I had tried to change. But she was running strong, staying with the leaders. I yelled, but she was too far away to hear.

Her legs pumped like pistons; her eyes aimed straight ahead; and she held at the center of the pack. She was running against great athletes, distance runners more gifted than herself. Realistically, I figured that when the race was over, Marcy would be in the middle, and therefore give our team much-needed bread-and-butter points.

First lap. The pain etched her face, the pain of 800 meters, but she still maintained her solid point-getting position.

Her mouth was dry and her eyes began to bulge. She thrust her arms out in front of herself to pick up speed.

Then it happened. She pulled a muscle in her left thigh. *Pain. Quit!*

She kept on running, even as her stride withered to a trot, then a limp, and finally a hobble.

Quit! a thousand voices screamed inside of her head. *Quit! Quit! Quit!*

One girl passed her. Another. Another.
Quit!
She was not the last person to finish. Two others trailed behind her. With determination, grit, and pain, Marcy had fought a myriad of forces that tempted her to give up. She stumbled over the finish line in tears.

After that race, I overheard one of our guys ask her, "Marcy, after you pulled that muscle, there was no way you were going to get team points. Why didn't you just quit?"

"Why didn't you just quit?" Those words ate right through me.

In the cold light of logic, in the passionless gray of the analytical mind, one can see the practical sense of Marcy dropping out of the race after pulling a leg muscle. After all, finishing the race would bring greater physical pain and no points. "Why didn't you just quit?"

But then I heard Marcy's answer: "Because my coach told me, '*Never* quit.'"

Marcy had put faith in my words: "Never give up. Try with all your might to finish the race, the project, the job, the mission that is before you." In my mind, Marcy became a district champion that day.

Your Turn

Do you remember the serpent and Eve in the Garden of Eden? Inside each of us there is a voice like the serpent's that whispers, "Why don't you just quit? Turn back to the world. Do you really have to be a Christian to be happy? Give up this Jesus business." That voice seems so reasonable. It's easy to follow that voice because sometimes it's the voice of your best friend.

But you must not listen to that voice. Your ears need to hear only the words of your Leader, the one who sets the higher standard.

Remember the words of your Leader when the temptations of the world pull at your muscles. Remember the words of your Leader when you feel pain, when the right thing seems too hard to do. Don't listen to the Enemy, who tells you that sin will help you. Remember the words of Jesus: "Follow me" (Mark 1:17, KJV).

"But they that wait upon the Lord shall renew their strength; they shall mount up with wings as eagles; they shall run, and not be weary; and they shall walk, and not faint" (Isa. 40:31, KJV).

1. Are others trying to convince you that certain activities are normal when the Bible calls them sin? Are they asking you to participate in sin?
2. What is pulling at you in your life now, making you feel pain in following Christ?
3. Has there ever been a time when you have wanted to quit a task you knew needed to be done?
4. Share about the times you have felt like quitting Christ. Can you see situations, people, and conditions you can avoid in order to strengthen your Christian life?
5. List the blessings you have received from following Christ. Do the blessings outweigh the pain?
6. What can you do both today and tomorrow that will be a safeguard against "pulled" spiritual muscles?

6

Whom Should I Listen To?

Rick was an exceptional athlete.

Working with him was a pleasant frustration. He had such talent it was difficult deciding where he would best be utilized. He was a fine sprinter, a good 800-meter man, and an excellent long jumper. But Rick's dream was to be a great pole vaulter. And I wanted to help him achieve his goal. Yes, Rick had a passion to be a pole vaulter, but he also had his eyes set on the school record in the long jump. At our next meet, I wanted to let him long jump in addition to his vaulting, but I knew he had been having leg troubles all season. He couldn't even compete in the sprint medley at our last meet.

It was the night before the meet; due to Rick's leg problem, I had a light workout for him. Rick soon completed the workout. I went into the locker room to talk to a shot putter. As Rick was cooling down, Jerry, last year's conference champion in the long jump, walked onto the field. He was back from college and was stopping by to help Rick.

"Hey, Rick!" Jerry called. "Hear you're going to long jump at conference."

Rick smiled. "I'd like to," he said and then laughed.

"Well, stretch out, I've got a workout all planned for you that'll make you conference champion."

Rick's mind saw the track record board in the school's trophy case; his dreams longed for each one of Jerry's words.

My coach said I should just do my workout and then shower. Rick thought. *I respect my coach, but was he ever the Maple*

Leaf Conference Champ in the long jump?

Rick's legs pounded into that long runway, his arms churning. The eyes of last year's champion tore into him as his foot hit the take-off board and he leaped high into the sky, with both feet shooting out before him, crashing into the wet sand. Rick struggled to his feet, and did the jump all over again. Then he sprinted and leaped again, and again.

Soaring. Almost touching the blue of the sky. Crashing to the soft earth. Sand in his mouth, his eyes, his hair. Again and again and again.

"Thanks, Jerry," Rick said, exuberance beaming from his face. "You helped me a lot. My speed and height and distance are better than ever."

The next day Rick hobbled out of bed. Walking was both painful and difficult. I sent him to a doctor that morning. The doctor warned Rick not to compete in the track meet, though it would be the most important of the season.

Jerry was a terrific athlete. He had the knowledge, kindness and talent to teach Rick many valuable lessons about long jumping. But Jerry was *not* Rick's *coach*. Jerry could only judge what was best for Rick from being with him for an hour. He had not watched and coached Rick for months. He did not have intimate knowledge of Rick's leg condition. Jerry had a shortsighted view of Rick as an athlete. He only visualized Rick as a long jumper who needed help in long jumping.

I had a farsighted view of Rick. I knew that pole vaulting was more important to him than any other event. I had been his coach for months, not just an hour. I knew what his strengths *and* weaknesses were, what part of his development needed the most attention and what was best to leave alone. I knew about his leg condition. And I knew the challenges ahead of him in the track season.

Your Turn

We often look at ourselves as Christians that need to be happy. We fail to understand that God has known our wants and needs before we were born. He knows our strengths and weaknesses better than we do, just as I, Rick's coach, knew him better than Jerry. He knows what will hurt us and He knows what's in our future. God can look at us through a microscope; we can't even see our own faces without first looking into a mirror, and that mirror distorts what we really look like.

The exhilaration that Rick got leaping high in the air ended in pain the next morning. God does not want to give us a happiness that lasts only an hour. As Rick's coach, I wanted him to have the joy of being conference pole-vault champion. So, too, God wants to give us great blessings. He wants us to have a happiness that is built upon a Rock, crafted by years of growth in Christ and the challenge of walking in the Spirit. He wants us to have a happiness that does not depend on our whims or on what is given or taken from us. He wants to give us a *durable* happiness that lasts throughout eternity.

The saddest sight of my first year of coaching was to look at Rick, not leaping and vaulting, but limping.

"For as the heavens are higher than the earth, so are my ways higher than your ways, and my thoughts than your thoughts" (Isa. 55:9, KJV).

1. Can you think of something that you felt you really needed? You asked God for it in prayer, and that prayer was not answered as you asked. Explain.
2. Can you think of any prayers that you were glad "weren't answered"?
3. Have you ever been angry at God for not answering a prayer in the way you wanted it answered?
4. What does it mean to you that God knows more about you than anyone else does?
5. How can we learn what God wants us to do with our lives?
6. What can you do right now that will make you more sensitive to what God wants you to do with your life? To trust God to satisfy your needs?

7

The Victory of Defeat

Kirk.

He was a short and stocky farm boy who had played football. Now it was the middle of the season and Kirk wanted to be a part of the track team.

He had a good build for a sprinter or a shot-putter, but I had sprinters, and I had shot putters. I needed an 800-meter runner.

The 800 is a tough race, so you need a strong desire to run it. Kirk may not have had the classic distance runner's build, but he certainly had the desire. So I worked with him, and Kirk trudged through the tedious practice sessions that would make him into an 800 man.

When Kirk began competition, he dug in and put out everything he had. He would come close to sprinting those two tough laps around the track. At every meet, Kirk would pull in a third or a fourth or a fifth place. Though he never took first place, he always came through with needed points to help his team; plus, he was building up the team's confidence.

But there was a saddened rage in Kirk's eyes when he was not chosen for the district relay team that would go to regions. His time was just not fast enough.

"Winning is a part of life," I told my team, "but so is losing. You can't be afraid of losing. Accept your defeat with courage and leave it behind you."

The night before district, Kirk walked out of the locker room with a duffel bag in his hand. My eyes met his. I could tell by his calm and sad humility that he had understood my words.

Two years later, just three days before another district track meet, I was walking the halls of the school. I stopped at the crossroads by the front doorway.

"Hello, Coach!"

I turned to look and saw a familiar figure in a soldier's uniform.

"Kirk! Good to see you." We shook hands.

He told me about the army; I told him about track. He had lots of questions about the school, the athletic program, and about the young men in the past that he had run against.

Kirk stood with a military erectness as he spoke. He grew quiet, swallowed, and at last said, "My brother just passed away."

Those five words sent a thousand visions hammering into me. In my mind I saw Kirk running hard, in a heartbreaking pace, struggling and sweating for a first place, but never receiving it. I saw his reaction when not chosen for the regions. That image was frozen in my mind. I looked at him. I could see a raging anger and a deep and hollow sadness. An anger because the good and the joyful times with his brother were forever lost. And a sorrow that screamed out, "I never told my brother that I loved him!"

His jaw quivered and I could see moisture forming in his eyes.

" . . . That's why I'm here on leave," he said. "It's rough."

His stark words made the halls of that school feel cold as a cave. Something deep within me ached. "I know," I said. "It's rough, Kirk." And that was all I could say.

My eyes went to the floor. I hope Kirk heard more in my words. Perhaps he heard that losing is a part of living. Everyone loses his physical life; everyone dies. Maybe when Kirk got all those third- and fourth-place ribbons, but never the blue number one, maybe those defeats prepared him in a small way for this great loss. Maybe failing to make the district relay team somehow molded him for this. *Could it be?*

But I was thinking small. My words were too trite. I was all wrong. *Nothing can prepare you for the death of a loved one. Nothing.*

But what about Christ? Christ gives eternal life, everlasting victory over death. I wanted to say something to Kirk that was more meaningful than, "It's rough." I wanted to say, "What about Christ? Do you know Jesus as a friend? Is He real to you now, Kirk? Now? Today? Can I tell you about Christ now?"

I lifted my head to speak to Kirk, but he had turned away. I watched him walk out the front doors holding his face in his hands. The heavy metal doors closed behind him with a sad finality.

Your Turn

Christ has defeated your last enemy, death, through His death. Without His death, there could be no life. Death is always near. Tell people about Christ *today*. Show your love to people *now*. Don't dwell upon death; dwell upon life, for true life is Christ.

"The last enemy that shall be destroyed is death" (1 Cor. 15:26, KJV).

1. Do you think experiencing loss in other areas of life prepares you for the death of a loved one?
2. If you were the coach, what would you have said to Kirk?
3. Is telling other people about Christ hard for you? Why?
4. What do you think can make witnessing for Christ easier?
5. To whom can you say "I love you" today and tomorrow?

8

Are Losers Forever?

Every meet, every race, all season long, he came in last. Dead last.

Wes always started out great in the mile. But by the middle of the race other runners started to pass him. And Wes would cross the finish line with a dry throat and a giddy exhaustion—in *last place.*

Meet after meet, it was always last place.

During one race Wes was *certain* another runner was behind him. When he stumbled across the finish line, he twisted his body around in desperation to see the first runner he had beaten. No one was there. Dead last again. Wes was always last. He never got a sixth-place ribbon because he was always behind sixth place. *When you're last you can say that you beat nobody.*

"Well, at least nobody's *somebody*," he'd laugh.

But when he went to the locker room to dress for a meet, he thought that he saw other eyes scorch into him. *Are they calling me loser?* he thought. *Are they mad at me because I don't bring in any points?*

He did his absolute best whenever he ran the mile. But at the end of each race, it was the same old story—dead last.

He pounded out mile after mile in practice. He was the hardest worker on the team, but he was always last place. *Last.* The word was branded into his soul.

And when the season ended, there were no ribbons, no letter, just an endless string of last places. By all rights, he could be called a "loser."

Summer. He lived with the self-proclaimed label of "loser." Fall. In his deepest heart he knew he was not a failure. Winter. *I wish I could show them now that I'm not a loser.* Spring. A new track season and a *new coach.*

"Hey, Wes, you going to run the mile this year?" asked Wendell, a teammate.

"Nope," answered Wes. "Not the mile. Two-mile."

"Two-mile? You crazy? You have a rough enough time running the mile. How're you ever going to run the two-mile?"

But I worked Wes hard and he did everything I asked him to without complaint. He ground out mile after mile of boring and painful practice. He fought aching muscles and sore feet and nausea, battling to erase an unspoken label branded upon him.

Our first track meet at Chatfield. Wes stood ready at the line. The gun!

Eight dreary laps stood mocking Wes as he elbowed his way toward the front of the pack. He struggled to stay at the front, and unbelievably, when he hit the mile mark, he was still at the front.

"Just four more laps!" I called. "Four more, Wes!"

Many people watching Wes on that day were guilty of asking themselves, "When will the others start passing him?"

But Wes fought to stay at the front.

Then, one runner passed him. Soon another young man shot in front of him. Then another.

The sight of those runners storming by him riddled his dreams. *Not this!* he screamed inside. *Not again.*

And he still had a half mile to go.

Another runner passed him. Then another. His throat was dry. His side ached. His body cried out: "Stop! Lie down!" But Wes kept beating the cinders, running hard. The summer, the fall, the winter had been too long.

His legs felt like cotton when he hit the last lap. His glasses slid to the end of his nose and almost fell off from the sweat.

But then I saw his face. I don't know how to describe that look, but I can tell you that it was not the look of a loser.

He set his face forward, eyes riveted into the back of the runners before him. And he plodded on, keeping the same pace for 100 meters.

Suddenly—Wes blasted forward! Speed fired into him. He

had an amazing resource of energy that made him, at that moment, the most powerful runner on that track. He pumped his arms; his face was explosive with determination.

He passed one runner. Another. Another.

Cheering pounded in his ears, cheering that he had not heard before. The finish line merged into a sea of colors, for he now gripped his glasses in his right hand. Wes didn't know how many bounded ahead of him, or how many lagged behind. But he knew he was not in last place. As he shot across the line, his teammates were there to catch him, and to congratulate him for winning third place.

Wes had learned something from his defeats in the mile: the mile was not his race. Many first-place ribbons were in his future.

Your Turn

If you can't make the choir, maybe that's a signal you should join the drama club. If you have not been successful in one line of work, perhaps there's another line you should be in. Maybe you have failed as an artist because God wants you to be a champion in something else.

Perhaps you lost one friend, so that you can go out and find another.

"But many that are first shall be last, and the last shall be first" (Matt. 19:30, KJV).

1. What is your response when you repeatedly fail at something?
2. Can you think of another person who failed at one task only to succeed at another?
3. What task have you repeatedly failed at? Do you think God is trying to show you something through that failure?
4. When is giving up one task to succeed in another bad?
5. List all the areas of your life in which you are a "winner."
6. What can you do tomorrow to turn from old failures to find new victories?

9

Disappointment

The doctor informed Rick that if he vaulted in the conference track meet, there was a strong possibility he would cripple his legs.

Track was Rick's favorite sport. He had taught himself how to pole vault as a kid. He had strained and sacrificed for years in order to achieve the goal of conference champion in that event, with hopes of going on to district, region, and state. All of these goals had been within his grasp, and now, with the doctor's prognosis, they vanished as mist before his eyes.

Rick was a senior. This injury had murdered his final year of high school track. With no plans for college, he was heartbroken and devastated.

Rick sat across from me in the office of the locker room. His head was bowed; the usual smile was missing from his face.

I needed to say something wise, something helpful. I prayed quickly for God to give me the words.

"Rick, sometimes we don't reach the goals we set for ourselves at the exact time we expect to achieve them. But that doesn't mean we won't someday achieve what we really want. No, you will never be the Maple Leaf Conference Pole Vault Champion. But you can use the pain that you feel now as a tool to help you achieve a much higher goal than that. Perhaps it's state champ, or an Olympic Gold Medal. Maybe you will be a great leader. Or become an outstanding coach. 'Conference Champ' would look very small compared to such accomplishments."

Rick's pained eyes penetrated into mine. We were both silent for a long time. Then, at last, I saw hope flicker in his eyes, a hope that I thought had turned to ashes. Hope soon turned into courage and the courage transformed itself into determination to conquer the future. Rick understood that trophies, medals, and championships do not always constitute victory in *God's* eyes.

Your Turn

Any misfortune that happens to us in this life God can turn to good. All things will be used for our benefit if we fit in with God's plans.

Dedicate your life to Christ. Ask Him to forgive your sins. Ask Him to guide and inspire you. Then whatever happens to you, even the shattering of your most cherished dreams, will be a masked blessing, which will one day give you joy.

"And we know that all things work together for good to them that love God, to them who are the called according to his purpose" (Rom. 8:28, KJV).

1. Can you think of a bad thing that happened in your life that turned into a good thing?
2. What does it mean to "love God"?
3. What does it mean to be "called according to his purpose"? (Check other Bible translations.)
4. How does Rom. 8:28 make you feel?
5. How can Rom. 8:28 be misused?
6. What can you do today and tomorrow to love God and to fit into His plan?

10

Her Father's Eyes

Lynn was a slender and graceful young woman, extremely co-ordinated, a natural athlete. Though only in tenth grade, she had hurdled for a number of years.

In the past, her father had worked with her at home on two hurdles, compassionately teaching, encouraging, and praising her with great patience. And today Lynn was extremely excited about the meet at Stewartville, her first regional track meet. She drank in all the color and the laughter and the anticipation.

"Beautiful day, isn't it, Mitch?" I said.

"Sure is," Lynn's father said. He was wearing sunglasses, and a stop watch hung from his neck. "Couldn't ask for a better day for a track meet."

"There might even be a little wind at Lynn's back," I said.

"That would help."

"Are you nervous?"

"Can't help it, I'm her father. And you?"

"I can't help it either, I'm her coach." We both laughed.

Then Mitch lowered his voice, his face showing solemn pride as he spoke to me. "She's sure done all right for herself. Getting up to regions as a sophomore in a tough region like this."

At the sound of the gun, he took off his sunglasses. I broke away from Mitch and elbowed my way through the crowd to get within shouting range of Lynn. I was tight against the fence.

I squinted down track in the direction of the starting line. I could see Lynn attacking the first hurdle; her form was perfect. Her feet hit the pavement and pounded the track, stride after stride to the next hurdle; perfect form again. But gliding off that next hurdle, her footing was uneven. She stuttered in her pace but soon regained balance and broke into her speed. She was not far behind the other leaders. Next hurdle? Perfect!

The cheering of the crowd had become an enormous wave pounding down on the runners.

The finish line! Not far away! If I can pass just two girls I'll be in the finals. Faster.

Next hurdle, perfect.

How did these other girls get so fast? she thought.

Next hurdle? Perfect. Step. Step. Step. *There's Dad! Dad . . .*

Her palms, her cheek, her side were all against the black surface of the track. The cheering had stopped—only silence. Lynn peered down the lane and watched the other girls finish the race without her.

In that split second, in that silent void of cold faces, she could see one face of warmth and love. She could see her father's eyes, and in those sad eyes she could also see the past: her father teaching her to ride a bike and coaching her in the long jump. She could see him helping her improve her spike in volley ball and her lay-up in basketball. And she could see her father struggling with her mathematics, helping her with her homework. Now before a frozen audience she was on her knees by the hurdle she should have conquered instead of tripping over.

Now I'm shaming you, Dad. Your daughter has failed.

But in that same moment she saw a face melted in love, not shame.

"If I could take away your pain, I would," her father's sad eyes said. "If only I could have been the one to fall and bear the stares of the crowd, I would. I would gladly bear your shame . . ."

The eternal split second ended when Lynn popped to her feet.

"Walk off the track!" the crowd shouted in her mind. "You won't make finals! Your time will *stink*!"

But what's there to be ashamed of? She looked down the lane. One hurdle stood between her and the finish line.

She bent over, flexed her leg muscles, and ran forward into the silence. And the crowd watched a young woman, with a dream in her eyes and great courage, clear a hurdle in perfect form and cross the finish line alone, without a hint of shame.

And I looked into the face of a very proud father.

Your Turn

God loves you infinitely deeper than Mitch loved Lynn. God's own Son suffered shame and pain for you, and was punished by death so that you could live.

"For God so loved the world, that he gave his only begotten Son, that whosoever believeth in him should not perish, but have everlasting life" (John 3:16, KJV).

1. In what ways does this story remind you of Jesus' crucifixion?
2. Does this story help you understand John 3:16?
3. Do you always finish the tasks that you start?
4. Can you think of some things you have started that should not be finished?
5. List some of the good things your parents have done for you.
6. What important, unfinished tasks can you finish today and tomorrow?

11

How Many Legs Does Rick Have?

Rick was a vital part of our team. And today was Maple Leaf Conference Track Meet.

We had been counting on Rick to grab first place in the pole vault, pull in at least a second place in the long jump, and to anchor a powerful 400-relay team. Now, without Rick, we would suffer a great deal. And I had just discovered from the doctor that Rick would not be able to compete in the district meet either.

I had to leave my desk in the coach's room and face my exuberant team, high on conquering the Maple Leaf, and tell them that Rick would not be vaulting, running, or jumping today.

I swallowed. I offered a quick prayer to God, needing His wisdom and His words. "Please speak through me, Lord, *please.*"

I could hear locker doors slamming, then laughter. In a momentary nervous silence, I sensed the excitement and the anticipation as I walked into the locker room.

"Can I have your attention?"

They were soon silent, looking at me as they laced up their shoes and put on their jerseys.

"The doctor says that Rick won't be able to compete today," I said. "We will be sadly lacking—"

"Boo hoo!" faked Wendell, hoping to get a laugh.

"Quiet!" I shouted. "Have you any idea what it's like to work for five years at being a champion pole vaulter and then have that championship robbed from you right at the point where you have a chance of making your dreams come true? Do you know how terrible that can be?"

The team was dead silent. I looked into their faces. I saw sadness, disappointment, frustration, and heartache.

"Rick can't use his legs today," I said. "So that means that we must be Rick's legs. Rick can't vault, so we have to use our determination to vault for Rick, to vault over this obstacle of having a weaker team than we had planned. We need to be Rick's arms to throw the discus and the shot farther than we ever have. We have to be a part of Rick's guts, and run each distance race with courage. We must be Rick's legs because he can't run and he can't jump. We need to break records and leap to new heights of achievement.

"We are Rick's legs and arms today. By doing our best, by struggling to do even more than our best, we will help give Rick his dreams. No, he will never be able to say that he is the Maple Leaf Pole Vault Champion, but he will be able to say that he is a part of a championship team."

The team astounded everyone with their power and courage and determination. They didn't win, but they scored high in the conference and in the district. The majority of the varsity squad went on to regional competition. The press, television, and radio took notice. There was power in the team's love for Rick and in teamwork. We didn't become the Maple Leaf Conference Champions, but we all understood true victory.

Your Turn

"People" are the twentieth-century Body of Christ. And if we are all a part of the Body, we must all work together and help each other.

You need to be the legs for the elderly man down the street who is too crippled to walk. Can you walk to the store for him? Or how about the blind girl? Can you be her eyes and read her the Bible?

You are Rick's legs, arms, and eyes.

My team found great power in doing something out of love for Rick. You can find joy in doing something out of love for God. Make your accomplishments witness to the power of the living God. Run your race for Christ, and you will know the wonder of godly victory.

But remember, don't run alone or against your brothers and sisters. We are all part of Christ's body and we need to help each other.

"For just as the body is one and has many members, and all the members of the body, though many, are one body, so it is with Christ" (1 Cor. 12:12, RSV).

1. When was the last time you helped a person for no reward? How did your kind act make you feel?
2. When you try to accomplish a worthy goal, for whom do you try to accomplish it? Some other person? God? Yourself?
3. Have you ever been someone's else's eyes, arms, or legs?
4. Read 1 Corinthians 12. Compare the Body of Christ to a human body. What part of the Body are you?
5. Think of examples of how a "weak" or "injured" member of the Body of Christ is important.
6. Who do you know that is discouraged and you can be his encouragement? Lonely and you can be her comfort? Sad and you can be their joy? Can you show love to these people tomorrow?

12

Faithful

The simplest way to describe the field event of shot put is to say that it is throwing a heavy iron ball as far as possible. But it's not really throwing; instead, the athlete pushes the shot out into the air with an arm.

Don was my number-one shot putter. Todd also was a shot putter and the same age as Don. Like Don, he was large and strong, a farm boy.

Todd came out for track on the first snowy day of practice. He lifted weights; he dreamed. He did his best in competition, but he did not get a single point all season. Yet he would not miss practice. He believed in himself. He struggled. I could *always* count on him to be at a track meet and give his best effort.

Todd was proud to be a part of the team. Proud that he could hurl the shot put farther than most people in Wykoff—or so he thought.

Toward the end of the season, a few weeks before district, Barry came out for track. He strolled into the locker room carrying his duffel bag, and plopped down on the bench next to Todd.

"What're you doing here, Barry?" Todd asked.

"I'm going out for track."

"Really? What are you planning on doing? You going to be a sprinter? You were fast in football. I bet you could be even faster on the track without all that equipment on—"

"I'm planning on throwing shot," Barry said.

"Shot?"

Todd's proud face sagged as his eyes sized up Barry's phy-

sique. He was bigger than Todd and his arms were more powerful. His speed and coordination were more refined.

It's not fair! Todd's heart screamed.

And on that night of practice, Barry stepped into the circle
and let that shot rest in the palm of his hand like a tennis ball.
He hurled it. And that first throw flew farther than Todd had
ever dreamed of throwing.

Todd huddled in the shadow of the school; a solitary tear
dropped from his eye. He nursed his wounded heart in silence,
wanting what was best for his team. But with each forceful toss of
Barry's shot put, another corner of Todd's hope and joy was
chipped away until nothing was left.

The roster sheet for the district track meet sat on my desk. In
each event I could enter only two people. This meant that some
people would not go on to district; the season would end for them
today.

When I got to "shot put," I wrote down Don's name first of
course. And for my second man, I wrote, Todd.

Your Turn

You may not have the talents of an Olympian or Beethoven.
But you have been given a ministry, a mission, and a purpose
that God wants you to carry out in this world.

Faithfully do the "small" things that God's Word asks you to
do. Share Christ with your family, friends, and community. Visit
the sick and the lonely.

If there are any "bigger things" for you to do for God, trust
God to lead you into them. Trust God, not your talent and ambition.

*"You have been faithful over a little, I will set you over much;
enter into the joy of your master"* ((Matt. 25:23, RSV).

1. Can you think of a situation where you felt threatened like
   Todd did?
2. Why did the coach pick Todd instead of Barry? Did he make a
   right decision?

3. Which does God honor more in a person, "faithfulness" or talent?
4. Do you ever cover up your laziness with natural talents?
5. What is your ministry?
6. What are some of the "small things" that you can do for God both today and tomorrow?

13

Sprinting to Lose

In one year, Wes had gone from being a loser in the mile to a regional competitor in the two-mile.

Wes lay awake at night visualizing the cheers and the glory.

If I could just get second place tomorrow, he thought, *I'll go on to state.*

The memories of being a loser in the mile seemed so long ago. "Last place" was in a mist of twisted nightmares trapped far away in his imagination.

I'm running in regions. Maybe I'll go on to state.

The next day, at the regional track meet at Stewartville, Wes was dazzled by the colors and the beautiful all-weather track. He was impressed by all the people in the stadium. There was a tingling excitement everywhere. *All these people will be watching me run. Me?*

Wes's lean body was ready to break out of the starting line. He had a black strap around his head to secure his glasses on his nose.

"Runners to your mark!"

I smiled at Wes. I too was thrilled to see him at regions.

Gun!

The runners were such a massive conglomeration that they had to run single file, doubled up in lanes, until they got the flag.

This is like running in a herd of cows, Wes thought.

But not cows, horses.

They're running too fast, Wes thought, as he struggled to keep up. *They're running like this is a half-mile, not a two-mile.*

But Wes fought to stay in the front for most of that first lap, attacking the track, running that lap faster than he had ever run before.

The speed was eating away at his endurance. Yet he could still delight in the bright colors. And he loved the mammoth crowd and the remarkable all-weather track at his feet. He remembered the joy of just being here, so he gritted his teeth and stuck it in hard for another lap.

But the other runners were starting to pass him. One by one, Wes heard each runner's calm breathing as he slipped past him, while West was left gasping for breath. He saw the strong, thick chords of muscles in their legs as they cut in in front of him.

These guys have been running the two-mile for years and years, Wes thought. *They've been training for this day ever since seventh grade. They can train year round. They don't have to do the farm work that I . . .*

Another runner passed him. Another. And *another!*

Fear gripped his inside. Wes remembered last year. He remembered coming in last place meet after meet and the dreadful feeling that came with "last place." He remembered the long summer, fall, and winter that he had waited through before he could prove himself.

But this is my last day to prove myself. Going into the army in a month. Is this how it's all going to end? In front of all these people? Last place?

Another runner passed him. And Wes could not see through the sweat and tears in his eyes. All vision blurred before him, and for a moment the track at his feet seemed like the clay track at Wykoff. And the massive crowd was a small handful of classmates. But his gut screamed out, "Last place!" *How could I ever have dreamed of state?*

Thump. Thump. Thump. His feet carried him on. Four more grueling, heartbreaking laps. Yet he was still running faster than ever, his present time his year's best.

The sweat and the tears cleared from his eyes and suddenly, his mind cleared as well.

I'm running at regions! I just started running this race in March and by May I'm in regions. Doing my best today will be my great victory. I'm at regions!

Again he felt the glorious all-weather track at his feet. He saw the gigantic crowd of cheering people, the bright colors.

Two people were still racing behind him when Wes went into his "kick." A deep reserve of energy exploded within him. He rocketed forward, moving faster and faster.

There was no chance for points, a ribbon, or a trophy. It was even too late to pass another runner, but Wes kicked it in, in the same manner he'd kicked it in when he won a race.

His feet beat into the track, his arms pumping, his face in pain. He sprinted it in with hope even though everything was hopeless.

Wykoff earned no team points that day. But Wes crossed the line a victor.

Your Turn

Sometimes it's easy to be discouraged. You want to serve God, but He puts you in many situations that appear hopeless.

Any task God calls you to do is not hopeless or He would not have called you. Any situation that God puts you in is not hopeless or He would not have put you there.

Therefore, it's important to rely on the Holy Spirit for that inner reserve of strength to do your best even in seemingly hopeless situations. Christ is our hope in *every* situation.

"In hope he [Abraham] believed against hope" (Rom. 4:18, RSV).

1. When an old fear returns to your life, what do you do about it?
2. Wes found hope when all was hopeless. Is such an attitude a virtue or an unrealistic delusion?
3. Has there ever been a hopeless situation in your life? What can you do?

14

Only You Can Defeat Yourself

We started track practice in March, in the gym, before the Minnesota snow had melted and spring beckoned us to go outside.

I piled the foam rubber padding so that Mattie would have a soft pit to drop upon and spaced the standards in front of the pit. "How high do you want the bar, Mattie?" I asked.

"Four feet," she barked out.

Four feet? She hardly looked four feet herself.

"You sure?" I asked.

"Yeah."

I set the bar at four feet.

She paused for a moment to look down at her white shoes. Then she dashed toward the bar and leaped, throwing one leg over it, then kicking her other leg into the air, she plummeted to the foam rubber—a perfect jump.

I didn't know a great deal about Mattie then. I knew she was Wendell's sister. I also knew that Mattie and her brother were new to the community. Her father had a job that required him to travel a great deal, so the family did not stay in one place for very long.

Mattie was extremely short. Her hair was cut short in a bob. She wore pop-bottle glasses and her teeth were slightly bucked. On her first day of school she had her fears like any new girl. But she was intelligent and possessed a natural sense of humor. She was also a gifted athlete. Many of the girls liked and respected Mattie. But for some strange reason Mattie didn't feel that she had many friends. She started to think she could gain respect, admiration, and friends if she became the "bad girl" instead of the "new girl."

Suddenly, the school watched a "Jekyll and Hyde" transformation. Mattie started talking loudly; she became brash and insulting. "It's good to cut someone else down before they cut you down," she said. She thought that she could get more attention if she was an indifferent student. Mattie soon started using her gift of humor for profanity and cruel jokes. Yes, she got laughter from other students, but it was always a nervous laughter. A sad laughter. And she had the suspicion the laughter was directed at herself.

One Friday I was walking down the hall when I noticed Mattie before her open locker.

"Hello, Mattie," I greeted her.

"Hi," she grunted.

Then I saw it. It was unmistakable. A deep disappointment and a cold sadness pierced me. Yes, I had seen it in her locker, though she quickly slammed the door shut.

"Mattie," I said.

"*What?*" she barked in a cruel defiance.

"What's in your locker?"

She looked around to see if others were near. No one. But she smiled and spoke sarcastically as if she stood before an audience of friends. "Oh, books, coat, lunch, track stuff . . ."

"Open the door, Mattie."

"Hey," she protested. "It's my locker, not yours—"

"Open the door," I repeated.

Reluctantly her pudgy fingers flung the door open in anger. A bottle of gin sat on the top shelf of the locker.

Mattie was declared ineligible and suspended from the track team. She avoided me after that escapade.

Another day I saw her walking alone in the hall. I stepped toward her. I wanted her to know that I didn't condemn her. I had been angry, but I had forgiven her. I wanted to tell her that when this period of ineligibility was over, there would be a place for her on the track team. I wanted her to know that though her crisis was a defeat, this defeat could be turned into a victory. *She* had turned victory into defeat, but now *she* had to do something positive about her defeat or it would remain a defeat. I wanted to tell her I believed in her . . .

. . . Then the bell rang. Students rushed out of the classrooms and Mattie was soon lost in the crowd.

Before I could talk to her again, she and her family moved out of Wykoff. I wondered if her defeat would forever remain a defeat.

Your Turn

God, in Christ, should be the main person from whom you seek friendship.

You can turn victory into defeat, but God can turn your defeats into victories *if you will let Him*. Give your defeats to God.

"And the victory that day was turned into mourning unto all the people" (2 Sam. 19:2, KJV).

1. Do you know anybody like Mattie?
2. Why does it seem that bad actions often get more attention than good?
3. Have you ever turned victory into defeat?
4. Have you ever been a "new girl" or "new boy"? How did you feel?
5. What is there about Mattie that you find in yourself?
6. What defeats can you give to God, trusting Him to turn those defeats into victories?

15

Dreams Never Die

The revelation that our team's size often made winning impossible really hurt. And Rick's injury hurt us as a team. In our conference and district, we felt like David battling a giant with a rock but no sling. Nevertheless, toward the end of my first year of coaching, I could say that three-quarters of my varsity squad was advancing past the district on to regional competition.

Three-quarters of our team wasn't very many. Yet it was a great number from our standpoint, and I was very pleased.

The second day of the regional track meet I drove the car to Stewartville. Riding with me was Warren, our miler, and the quarter-mile relay team: Goldie, Jamie, Johnny, and Reed. All were competing at regions for the first time.

"We're going to have to make sure that we practice that blind baton pass so that we get it down *smooth*," Johnny said excitedly. And the rest of the relay team agreed with anticipation.

"Yes," I said. "The smoother you pass that baton the more seconds you'll knock off, and the better the time."

Jamie leaned over the front seat, bringing his face close to my ear. This was his first year in track; he had just moved up from Alabama. "We're going to get 'em," he drawled. "We've got the speed. We're going to do great."

I sensed that Jamie's dreams were no longer faint whisps, but stood before him as solid reality.

Goldie, Jamie's friend, with a blond crop of hair, shot up in the car seat. "Yeah. I'm surprised we got this far," he said. "But I believe more in our speed now. We have to get that relay team from La Crescent, the one that beat us in district."

"We've been working on our baton exchanges all week," Johnny piped in. "We've got 'em down *smooth*. That might give us an edge over the other teams. Who knows? The top team in the region might drop their baton and we might benefit from their mistake." He was talking fast, eager to prove himself on the track.

Warren was sitting in front next to me. He held a medal from district in his hand. "I'm proud of this," he said. "And I'm going to put everything into my race today. Who knows, Coach? Maybe I can get me an even bigger medal today."

Excitement bubbled inside our car. *We were going to regions. A step before state. Not every coach can say that.*

The 400-meter relay teams were ready for takeoff.

The gun!

Goldie dug into the track, clutching the baton. He ran with pain showing in his face, building up speed in the outside lane. He spotted Jamie.

Jamie's hand fired back as he started his run. Goldie slapped the baton into Jamie's palm, and he quickly wrapped his fingers around it.

Jamie's face shouted: "I'm running for my God! My girlfriend! My team! Myself!" He handed off to Reed, and Reed beat into the track, drowning in the shouts of the crowd. Reed soon slapped the baton into Johnny's left hand.

Johnny's face wrinkled in his last race as a high school trackman. He forgot all about form, his arms whipping wildly. He ran with pure force, pure speed, pure strength, rushing for the tape. Dreams and goals were still alive. The spirits of three young men and all of Wykoff were perched upon his shoulders. He squeezed the baton so tightly that the tips of his fingers were white. Johnny blasted across the finish line, but his quarter-mile relay team did not advance to the finals.

No one from Wykoff scored points at regions.

After the meet, some of my trackmen rode home with family and friends. My team was physically breaking up, each member going in a different direction. And why not? The season was over.

I still had the school car. But the only people riding back to Wykoff with me on that warm spring day were Goldie and Jamie. As we walked to the car in the parking lot, I wondered if Wykoff could ever advance past regions. Could Wykoff ever surmount all the obstacles and be known as a track school? Should I come back next year as coach? Is it worth the pain and the worry? Would anyone even come out next year? Maybe I had been unrealistic. I had dreamed of taking the team to state. Now I had to face the bitter fact that my dreams would not come true.

I pulled into a root-beer stand in Spring Valley.

What do I say to a team now that the season's over? What do I say to a team of two that was once a team of twenty-seven? What do I say to two young men who believed my preaching that they could be winners? What do I say to them now that their dreams won't come true?

"We dreamed big," I said. "At least we tried with all we had to gain a big victory. And aren't we better off failing at winning a big victory than conquering a puny victory, a tiny victory, that doesn't stretch our courage, our hopes, and our dreams? We tried to win the big victory. We failed, but aren't we better off for trying?"

Silence gripped our car as both of the young men sipped their root beers.

"We'll get 'em next year," Jamie said.

Your Turn

Many victories are called failures in the eyes of the world. But victory is doing anything that is God's will. Ask God to burn that thought into your mind so that you *never* forget it.

Dare to do big things for God, and your failures can always be victories.

"These all died in faith, not having received what was promised, but having seen it and greeted it from afar, and having acknowledged that they were strangers and exiles on the earth" (Heb. 11:13, RSV).

1. Look at the coach's last statement. Do you agree?
2. Think of the last time that you failed at a big task. What positive benefits did you get from that failure?
3. What is your biggest dream?

4. Does your biggest dream fit in with God's will according to the Bible?
5. Is failure a necessary part of life?
6. What big goals can you start to achieve today?

16

Not Enough

Mid-March, a new track season, and my second year of coaching. But this year my responsibilities would be compounded. I would be in charge of both the boys' and girls' teams. Warren and Wes had both graduated. I had no distance runners.

Kelly was one of many new faces that season.

He was tall and lean with long legs, and physically strong. But what was more important, he told me that he really wanted to be a distance runner.

I issued to him a sweat suit; he purchased a pair of track shoes. He was hungry to put miles under his feet and be a part of the team. His desire was to be a two-miler. After his first tough workout he asked me, "Coach, could you write up a workout for me to do after supper tonight and on weekends?"

"You want to be a distance man, don't you?"

"Sure do," he answered with conviction.

Suddenly there was another young man at my side. Darren. "Make me out the same schedule," Darren said. His voice was firm.

Darren did not have the build of a distance runner. He was too stocky. But he had desire, and he wanted to be a miler. In fact, he had more "desire" than anyone else on the team. Darren had a unique combination of both endurance and speed. When he ran, "desire" flooded every fiber of his being. In practice he'd run full force, not caring about how he would feel after the run, only caring about being victorious.

Kelly, on the other hand, ran with perseverance. He would

look at the distance his workout called for, and then he would methodically and strategically pace himself, gradually building up speed. While he ran, Kelly was molding the mindset necessary for a calculated victory over his opponents. He knew that he would have to adapt to the pace of the lead runner and stay with that runner in order to beat him. "I want to be a two-miler with all my guts," Kelly said. "I want to be a part of the team." And the first meet was now only a week and a half away.

"Coach," Kelly said with Darren at his side, "could you make up a workout for us this weekend? We want to run together."

"It's good for you guys to run," I said. "But be careful. Running too much on hard surfaces can be dangerous, especially if you don't warm up properly."

"Don't worry," Darren said. "We're going to be your best distance men."

The two young men ran hard. Desire and Perseverance in sweats and track shoes. They battled aching muscles, parched throats, and nausea so that they could be part of a great team.

One day Kelly put in some rough miles on a hard road and after showering, noticed a sharp pain in his leg. The next morning his mother sent him to the doctor.

On another day, Darren was doing chores on the family farm. As he lugged a hay bale, he felt agony in his knee from an old injury. His father sent him to the doctor the following afternoon.

The season's first track meet.

Kelly watched the running, the vaulting, the throwing, and the jumping wearing a cast and leaning upon crutches. Darren sat and watched, frustrated that he could not run for two months. Life seemed to be playing a cruel prank. Kelly had calculated how to stride victoriously through races, but he had not calculated how to pace his private conditioning. Darren's desire was great, but that desire could not conquer bruises of the past. Desire and perseverance aren't enough.

Kelly was on crutches until the day he graduated. He patiently maneuvered throughout the halls of school, limping from class to class. He strategically plotted the future, desiring to bury this defeat with a great victory.

Darren's desire seethed inside of him for the rest of the season. He waited anxiously for the two-month period to be over so that he could run at the district track meet. Darren planned that if the doctor gave him the "go ahead," he would work out for a couple days. And then he would run his heart out at the district, with no thought of the future.

The smell of the doctor's office and the feel of the cold metal against his skin sickened him.

"Can I run at district?" Darren asked the doctor.

The doctor studied Darren. Later he would remark that this young man was a bomb about to explode. A champion.

"I'm sorry, Darren," the doctor replied. "No running for at least another month." The voice was so final, so detached, so lonely.

Your Turn

There are many noble virtues: perseverance, courage, thrift, modesty, kindness. But these virtues aren't enough. In fact, they are *nothing* unless they are attached to love. And the Apostle John says that "God is love." So everything in your life is not enough for true life unless Christ is your life. You are nothing without love. God is love. And Christ is God.

"If I . . . have not love, I am nothing" (1 Cor. 13:2, RSV).

1. "Desire" summed up Darren. "Perseverance" summed up Kelly. Name one word that sums up you.
2. What positive lessons do you think these two young men can learn from their disappointments?
3. Do you have one talent or gift from God that you use without love?
4. How can we do all things with love?
5. Describe a time that you saw true love in action.
6. What one new thing can you do in love tomorrow?

17

How Can I Heal Yesterday?

She had gone out for track for many years. And her speed amazed her parents, her teammates and her opponents. Wendy had unbelievable speed, a natural talent. Everyone waited for the day when her talent would combine with work and maturity, and she would dazzle all eyes at the state track meet.

Wendy was the daughter of a prominent dairy farmer. She worked hard and possessed many talents. She was pretty and her voice was always pleasant and encouraging. Lettering year after year, she had collected a pile of ribbons and trophies. But for some reason, she decided during her junior year that she was not going out for track.

"Wendy, how come you're not going out for track this year?"

"I don't want to," she said. "I'm too involved with other things—studies, farm work, Prom."

Then in her senior year, Wendy wanted to go out for track. Her first race.

"Runners to your mark! Set!" Gun shot!

Wendy exploded out of the blocks. But Sandy blasted ahead of her. So did Tia. Girls she had beaten two years ago now over-whelmed her. *And what about that girl from Grand Meadow? And the one from Spring Valley? How did they get so fast?*

Wendy put everything into that race, only to get a third place. The strength she had built up in four seasons of track had slipped because of one season of inactivity. But her opponents, through last year's training and competition, had improved.

"I wish I would have gone out last year," she said. "Maybe I can't rest on my talent. I can't coast on past accomplishments."

"You made a mistake, Wendy," I said, "but now it's behind you. What are you going to do with your mistake? Let it defeat you? Let it make you wallow in guilt? Or do you leave it behind you and look up and run forward?"

"Track isn't God," she protested. "I didn't go out last year because I had more important things to do than track."

Whenever she would show up at a track meet, the girls from the other teams would recognize her, remember her speed, and their eyes would rip into her, demanding a perfection that she didn't have.

Yet when Wendy would leave a meet with just a third-place ribbon, voices would say, "Too bad that Brooks lost her talent. Remember when she was fast?"

What could she do? She felt the frustration of the "now" as she saw the glories of her past. So she worked, and she struggled hard. She followed every word I told her to try to regain her precious speed.

And one day the speed that had amazed and dazzled Wykoff in the past returned to her present. She scored high in the 100 at the district. She went on to regions, and flashed through the qualifying race to advance to the finals.

Counting Wendy, there were eight young women at the starting line. Six would place, and two would go on to state.

Gun shot!

The 100-meter race is over before you know it has even started. When the smoke of the gun cleared and the tape was broken, I knew that Wendy was not going to state. She would not even take home a ribbon.

I walked her to her parents' car.

"There's got to come an end to winning sometime," I said. "If you would have gone on to state and beaten everybody there, and then gone on to national competition and beaten everybody there, and then gone on to the Olympics . . ." She laughed. ". . . And beaten everyone there," I continued, "one day, somebody, somewhere, would have beaten you. You're winning can go only so far, Wendy. So you do your best and accept wherever your winning stops as victory. You should look back at your past victories with a sense of accomplishment, but you should never let your past victories control you, or make you content, so that you don't want to go on to new victories."

Her mother and her dad were waiting for her by their car. They almost glowed with pride.

"Wendy, I'm very proud of you," I said quickly. "You refused to let a mistake cripple you. You worked hard. You did your best and you advanced further in this region than anybody from Wykoff ever has."

She jumped into her parents' car, and as they drove away, she said, "I wish I would have gone out for track last year."

And although that car was full of people, it seemed very empty inside.

Your Turn

All people have regrets. *You* have regrets, and sometimes they come back to haunt you like unwelcomed ghosts.

It's important that you put your regrets into God's hands and trust Him. He wants to use your past regrets to help build your future, according to His good and perfect will.

"This one thing I do, forgetting those things which are behind, and reaching forward unto those things which are before, I press toward the mark for the prize of the high calling of God in Christ Jesus" (Phil. 3:13, 14, KJV).

1. What is your biggest regret in life?
2. If you "could do something different" in your life, what would you do?
3. What did you learn about regrets in this story?
4. Are your regrets connected with past sins?
5. Is there any relationship between a regret that you may have now and your refusal to repent of a sin to God?
6. What can you do both today and tomorrow to deal with your regrets constructively?

18

The Only Cure for Anger

Another track meet at Spring Valley. This time I thought we were going to win. A real, honest victory. The taste would be so sweet.

While anchoring the 400-meter relay, Jamie pulled a muscle in the thigh of his right leg. Jamie was the fastest sprinter in the district this year. Now he was rolling on the ground, clutching his leg in agony. I felt so helpless.

Goldie massaged the injured leg. I got Jamie up walking, then jogging a little. He tried to run, but it was no use. It would be too dangerous.

"Coach, I've got to leave for my motorcycle test," said Reed in the middle of the hustle, the excitement, and the pain.

"Huh?"

"I've got to leave now," Reed said.

"I thought that test wasn't for an hour yet."

"Yeah, but I thought that it would be good for me to get there early. I think my mom and dad would like that."

I remembered that he had mentioned the day before how important it was to take his motorcycle driver's test. He needed to drive his motorcycle to work; it was his only form of transportation. But the testing could be done only on a certain day, at a certain time; and the testing place was miles from this track meet.

"You'd better wait awhile, and tell me before you go," I said.

But all Reed heard me say was the word "go." He backed away, almost in a run. "Okay, Coach. Okay. Anything you say . . ."

Jamie had been a big hope for our team. And he was well-liked and respected by his teammates. He had moved up from Alabama just last year. His soft southern accent and Southern Baptist theology seemed strange to us Minnesota Lutherans, but the fact that he was unique helped his popularity. He was pleasant, polite, helpful, friendly, and intelligent. He was also my best sprinter.

He had won the 100-meter earlier that day. It seemed to me as if Jamie had been running in place until he reached the 70-meter mark. And then, all others had dropped behind him. Jamie had leaned forward with his chest and broken the tape—the winner! But Reed had been right at his heels in second place.

Reed. Strong and talkative Reed. He would be the one to replace Jamie in the upcoming 200-meter dash. Yes, it would be better if both young men were running the race for more points; but Reed, sprinting the 200, and the mile relay, might give us enough points to pull this meet off yet.

The 200 came, and Reed was not in the starting blocks. Pete, a sprinter and long jumper, ran up to me. "Reed's gone; he left for that test," he said.

"I told him not to leave until I said so."

Pete's bright eyes flashed in anger. "We could have won this meet if he would have stayed and helped us," he sparked.

Peter turned into a prophet, though I didn't want his words to come true. We did lose the track meet. And I thought the team I had worked so hard to build was crumbling right before my eyes. Jamie had injured his sprinting ability, and the whole team lost their sense of unity because they were mad at Reed.

The next day I was in the principal's office.

"There seems to be a lot of hostility among the trackmen," Mr. Thomas said. "Hostility against Reed. That attitude is harming the learning climate of the entire school. It's creating an ugly spirit between Reed and the rest of the students. I'm afraid of what might happen here in school—an open hostility."

"Yes, I know that, Mr. Thomas. But Reed's not to blame. It's my fault."

"Well, this problem developed at a track meet, and it's crossed over into the classroom. I feel you can do the best job patching it up. You're the track coach."

Yes, it was my fault. But the team had to give up its anger

against Reed before it could forgive me.

I knew exactly where I had to go first.

I dashed up to the third floor and stuck my head into the math class. Soon Jamie was out in the hall. This wasn't a job a coach could do alone. I needed help.

"Jamie. We have to think of forgiveness. The team needs to forgive both Reed and me. It's our duty as Christians."

Jamie looked at me long and hard. A wide smile crossed his face, he nodded his head. Then the bell rang.

I rushed down the flight of stairs and caught Pete by the arm between classes.

"Pete. Please forgive me . . . "

Two young men, leaders of the track team, found it in their hearts to forgive. As leaders, they were able to lead a majority of the team to forgiveness.

Unity soon returned because Jamie and Pete found the courage to forgive.

Your Turn

Sometimes forgiveness is the only action that can restore unity in a friendship, marriage, family, school, team, or business. Forgiveness is from God, and is a universal principle for successful living.

I don't care what a person has done to you, forgiveness is necessary in doing the will of God. Therefore, forgiveness is not for the weak-willed but for the courageous. If you find that you can't forgive, remember that Jesus can forgive any person through you.

"So you should rather turn to forgive and comfort him, or he may be overwhelmed by excessive sorrow" (2 Cor. 2:7, RSV).

1. Do you think forgiveness is important to God? If so, why?
2. What is the most difficult part about forgiving another person?
3. Do you know another person who won't forgive you? How does this make you feel about forgiving others?
4. If someone won't forgive you, what can you do to encourage his forgiveness?
5. Whom can you forgive today?

19

What If God Drops the Baton?

The shot was heard far away.

Energy and excitement gripped the girls. They wanted to win this track meet. They were passionate in their tasks and raucous in their cheering, screaming for their teammates until their voices rasped. The team's last hope was in the 400-meter relay squad: Janie, Sherri, Sandy, and Sally. We all hoped this crew would bring in big points, giving us a needed boost in the track meet.

Janie dived out of the blocks, her speed pumping up, her legs cranking faster with each step.

Four people would carry the baton. Sally, the last person, had the speed and power to make up for any lost ground. The other three girls, as well as the whole team, depended upon Sally.

Sally looked behind her and saw Janie pass off to Sherri. Nearly perfect. Sherri's strong legs were blasting forward.

We're tied for the lead, Sally thought. *I'd rather that our team be behind when the baton's handed to me. Then I have an excuse for not getting first place.*

The baton was slapped into Sandy's hand. Wykoff was now commanding the lead.

Sally wiped the sweat off her hand onto her uniform. *So nervous*, she thought. *Don't mind a dash or the high jump, but when three others depend on me, that's when I get nervous.*

She could hear Sandy's footsteps pounding behind her. Sally's eyes scorched into the crowd; she could see and hear her teammates calling her name. *Those three depend on me. My team depends on me.*

Sandy was almost there. Sally began her sprint within the exchange zone. Sandy entered the zone, and Sally's arm shot back. Sandy slapped the baton down. Sally could feel the hollow tube in her hand, her fingers wrapped around it. And then, she felt the baton slip away from her.

The clatter of the baton hitting the all-weather track fired into Sally's ears. For a moment she panicked. The opposing runners stormed past her. Hey! The baton was still lying in the exchange zone.

Sally scooped up that baton and ran her fastest race ever. But her relay team came in last place.

Your Turn

Your work for God is not independent. It's dependent upon Christ and the people that make up Christ's Body on earth.

Sometimes people fail us, and we become angry with them. People are imperfect, and they *do* fail. Only God is perfect. He will never fail.

"Be strong and of good courage, do not fear or be in dread of them: for it is the Lord your God who goes with you; he will not fail you or forsake you" (Deut. 31:6, RSV).

1. Who are the people that you are dependent upon?
2. In what ways are you dependent upon God?
3. If you were a member of that relay team, what would you say to Sally after the race?
4. Have you ever let anyone else down? How did you feel?
5. Are you ever afraid of responsibility?
6. What can you do tomorrow to increase your sensitivity to your dependence upon God?

20

Where Can I Find a Rustproof Hero?

He had many heroes. And his heroes were all a part of the track team.

There was Reed. The strong one who believed no enemy could stop him from achieving his goals. One who had the courage to believe God's vision of what he should be.

Jamie. The symbol of faith.

Goldie, he had the strength to laugh. And his laughter said that despite the hardships and the wounded expectations, somehow, in the end, everything would be mended and healed. His jokes were told in the laughter of faith.

Then there was Darren, who ran the mile. A person to be esteemed and respected.

How about Don, the shot putter, and the pole vaulter, Rick? They were brave enough to pick up the pieces of broken dreams and use those pieces to construct new dreams. These two young men, standing beside Darren, shined as profound examples that no one needs to remain defeated.

There was Kelly, the two-miler, who could use a handicap as a teaching tool to enrich his life. Todd, who threw the shot put and believed in doing his best. Sam, the hurdler, who strived for excellence at all times. And Kirk, the stocky 800-meter man, who could, with courage, confront life's most bitter tragedies.

Yes, Wendell had many people whom he looked up to. He wanted to be like them. But he wanted to resemble his heroes the most by being a hero in the eyes of someone else.

So he worked hard and sprinted his best at track meets in

hopes of becoming a hero. But day after day passed, and no one called him "hero."

Wendell was practicing his starts out of blocks in the back of the school. On this warm day, he positioned himself in the blocks and was ready to dive out of them when suddenly he was covered by a small shadow. Wendell looked up to see a small nine-year-old boy, Burkie. The boy who always wore a big brown stocking cap—even on warm days.

"Wha'cha do'n, Wendy?" Burkie asked.

Wendell lowered his hips. He was now on his hands and knees as he glared into the boy. "*Don't* call me 'Wendy,' " he said sharply.

Burkie was hurt. "Why not?"

"Because there's already a 'Wendy' on the team, and she's a girl . . ."

With a huffing indignation, Wendell remounted the blocks, raised his hips, and shot forward, sprinting fifty yards. Jogging back, Wendell noticed that Burkie was watching him intently, his mouth wide open and his eyes as big as saucers.

Wendell quickly mounted the blocks again. Then he dove out of the blocks in a fine theatrical copy of Reed's last race. After running fifty yards, Wendell looked over his shoulder and saw Burkie still watching him as though in a trance close to worship.

Wendell put his hands on his hips and feigned a slight limp as he walked over to the boy. He wanted to show, like Kelly, that he could surmount injuries.

"How'd you get so *fast*?" Burkie asked.

Wendell put his fingers to his chin, thought a moment, and then said, "I pray every night, and ask God to help make me fast." *Isn't that something that Jamie would say?*

The boy gulped and watched Wendell get into the blocks for another time.

"Do you always start your runs with blocks?" Burkie asked.

"No," Wendell said. "Not when I run the 400, you know, Goldie's race. Or the 800, the event that Kirk is always in." He exploded out of the blocks, and as Wendell's feet pounded the sand, Burkie's eyes just about popped out of his head. He sprinted up to Wendell and gripped his arm.

"If I pray, will it make me fast too?" Burkie blurted out.

Wendell looked down at the boy, fully appreciating all this

admiration. Then he thought of Sam. "You've got to work too," he said. "And strive to be excellent." He thought of Don and Rick. "You can't let disappointments stop you if you want to be fast like me. You've got to defeat your disappointments." He remembered Darren. "You have to want to be a trackman, and work real hard at it." *Todd.* "And you have to do your best and be faithful to the team."

Burkie nodded his head vigorously, worried that he would not be able to take in all the vital information Wendell was feeding him.

Wendell pointed to the mud and clay track. "We're going to have a track meet here tomorrow," he said. "Why don't you come and watch me run? Maybe I can teach you a few things."

"*Really?*" Burkie said, delighted and enchanted. "Me?"

"Yeah." Then he remembered Rick and Jamie's modesty. "Maybe I won't do so good against all the competition, but you can still learn something from my defeat." He laughed just like Goldie.

"Oh, I'm sure you'll be a champ." Burkie's face beamed.

And that small boy did go to the track meet. Wendell did not win anything, but he impressed Burkie. At the end of the meet, the boy ran up to Wendell. "I want to be just like you," he said.

But who am I? the older youth wondered. *An actor who pretends that I'm all my heroes?*

The conference meet was near. At this meet Wendell believed he could gain hero status with himself. *Maybe I'll be able to win the 100. Or at least get a second place.*

Burkie had no doubts about how Wendell would do. He announced to his teachers and to his whole third-grade class that his hero was going to win the 100-meter dash at the conference meet. And when he, Burkie, was Wendell's age, he too would win that race.

Burkie pleaded with his parents, and at last they gave in. Yes, they would drive him over to Spring Valley and the three of them would watch the Maple Leaf Conference Track Meet as a family.

The small boy was close by every night at practice when Wendell worked out. And the trackman thoroughly enjoyed having this fan watch him.

Burkie ran from one corner of the backyard to the other, trying to remember all the gems of knowledge Wendell had told him about championship. He soon found out that hard work and desire and courage were applicable in other tasks also. Burkie soon improved as a student.

Burkie could not sleep the night before the conference meet. The excitement was too intense. But he did pray. He prayed that one day he too could be fast. And he also prayed for Wendell.

Before his parents picked him up from school, he was bragging to a crowd of classmates how Wendell was going to beat both Jamie and Reed today. And in the hurried ride over to Spring Valley, Burkie chattered incessantly about his hero.

"I'm eager to see this young man run," his father said, as he pulled into the parking lot near the track. "We made it, Burkie. Just in time too. Looks like the 100's about to start . . ."

The family jumped out of the car. Burkie grasped the hands of his mother and father and pulled them behind him; they all ran toward the track.

Gun shot!

The 100 was starting. The boy broke away from his parents, ran through the crowd of people, and slammed into the fence, his nose against the mesh.

All he could see was the finish of the race.

C'mon, Wendell! That's it! Wendell is . . . no? Wendell is . . . no? Wendell?

His hero was not in fourth place. And he was not in third. Wendell was not in second place. He was . . .

. . . Not in the race at all. He was nowhere to be seen. Not at any of the field events. Not in the crowd of teammates. Not in the bus. Nowhere.

Burkie took off his brown stocking cap and wiped the tears from his face.

Days later, Burkie bumped into someone at school.

"Wendell."

" . . . I couldn't keep up the grades. I'm ineligible for track. Look, I'm sorry. Aw, why do you have to be so young? I feel like I'm talking to my starting blocks. Can't you understand that nobody can be a perfect hero? *Nobody.*"

Then Burkie looked up so that Wendell could see his face. Wendell saw terrible confusion. Burkie could not understand why a young man who talked about God and discipline and excellence could fail so miserably. Burkie's whole world had collapsed. Burkie had lost a hero.

The young boy turned violently away from Wendell, storming down the hall. As Wendell watched the brown stocking cap move farther and farther away, he felt ill.

What's happening? My sister's got a drinking problem. I'm off the team. My dad's moving us out of town. I'm losing a friend.

Wendell swallowed, choking on his sadness within. Then abruptly, he sprinted down the hall, ripped around the corner, and grabbed a frightened Burkie by the arm just as the boy was reaching for his coat on a hook.

"Listen," Wendell said firmly, "I'm glad I let you down 'cause I was leading you down the wrong road. I'm no hero. You shouldn't look up to me. Copy me and you'll end up hurting yourself bad . . . "

Burkie tried to run away, but Wendell gripped his arm.

"It's okay for you to have heroes," Wendell said. "Go to track practice tonight and get some new heroes. Learn from your heroes, but don't get so tied to your heroes that you want to *be* them. Learn from Jamie's faith and Goldie's laughter and Don's courage. But don't expect anybody to be perfect."

Wendell let go of his arm. Burkie stood silently, his face showing no sign of understanding. But Wendell knew that one day, when the boy was older, he would *remember* the words.

And as Burkie walked away from him, Wendell sighed. For the first time he felt a little like a hero. Burkie's prayers for Wendell had been answered.

Your Turn

Your heroes will always let you down because you set them up too high. You have made your heroes play roles that only God can play.

Forgive your parents and teachers and leaders, for none of them are perfect. Forgive your heroes. But remember, the only true hero is Jesus Christ.

Let the Spirit of God guide your life so that if anyone seeks to know Christ's character by looking at you, he will not walk away cursing God.

"They are exalted for a little while, but are gone and brought

low; they are taken out of the way as all other, and cut off as the tops of the ears of corn" (Job 24:24, KJV).

1. Can you think of a time when someone you trusted disappointed you? Explain.
2. Who is your hero?
3. Does this story make you more understanding toward the failures of those whom you look up to?
4. Is it ever right to put another person on a pedestal?
5. What's the difference between "having a hero" and "hero worship"?
6. What responsibility do you have to the younger people who look up to you? In what ways can you carry out that responsibility tomorrow?

21

Can a Winner Lose?

"I hate that race!"

The tri-captain always said that before the 400. And he always said that after the race, between the gasps and the agony.

He detested the 400, but he always ran it magnificently. He was my very best quarter-miler. In fact, his name was synonymous with the 400.

We called him Goldie because of the blonde crop on top of his head. Goldie loved to joke. He would brag about an "A" on a poem he had written for English class. The poem was about the 400 and how much he hated losing dinner after that race. Yes, he made the team laugh, and he rarely complained. He always did what I told him to do.

The 400 seemed like it would be easy to run. Just once around the track. And it *would* be easy if you walked it, or jogged it. But the 400 could be won only if you sprinted the whole race. There's a point around the 250-meter mark where the runner feels as if he's hitting a brick wall. He has no more wind. No more endurance. No more strength. His eyes bug, and his legs are so heavy he can hardly lift them. When the runner finally breaks the tape, he usually has nausea, fainting, or utter exhaustion to look forward to.

After a quarter mile, I'd usually find Goldie behind a building, bent over, feeling ill. But Goldie won races. He won *every* 400-meter race I put him in. Goldie knew the cheering of his teammates. He knew the cheering of large crowds and he knew the cheering of small crowds. He heard the cheering until it roared in his ears.

He had a bulletin board at home filled with first-place ribbons and newspaper clippings. At the end of every season he was the school record-holder in the 400. And each succeeding season he would break his own record.

Goldie was proud of his school record. He would stand in front of the school's trophy case after practice, duffel bag tight in his hand, his breath fogging the glass, reading and re-reading his name for the record he set in the race he dreaded running.

But pain could rip into Goldie too.

He had had kidney troubles as a child. And now, in his senior year, there was a flare-up of this old problem. Back pains made running torturous. Though it was his last season, I did not give him difficult workouts, and he did not run at many of the meets. Instead, he watched from the sidelines.

"Hey, Goldie, I'm running for you today," Reed said as he dropped beside Goldie on the grass and began his stretch exercises.

"Wish I was running," Goldie said. "I want to make sure that I break my record this season."

Reed looked up from the grass and grinned. "You're going to have to break my record then," he said.

"Aw, c'mon . . ."

"I'm going to break your quarter record today," Reed said.

"The *first* time that you run it? Quit pulling my leg, Reed."

Moments before the race, I said to Reed, "When you hit the second to the last curve, it's going to feel like a brick wall. If you're behind anybody at that point, pass them going into the curve. It sounds crazy, because most runners conserve their energy running a curve and then go all out after the curve. But I'll tell you a secret, use all your energy to get ahead of them then. They'll be so tired after hitting the "brick wall" that there's a ninety-five percent chance they'll never pass you again."

Reed looked down at the ground and nodded his head. Confidence welled up inside. "Anything you say, Coach," he said.

"Last call for the 400-meter dash!"

All the runners lined up. Reed did not use blocks; he was bent over, the muscles in his legs strained. Determination was written on his face.

Gun shot! Reed was in the lead as the runners pounded out

the first 100 meters. I watched each second tick by on my stop watch. And then I squinted toward the "brick wall." Reed was well ahead of everyone.

Goldie saw Reed's confident, smiling face heading for the tape. Goldie saw that Reed, a younger athlete, was far ahead of everybody. Goldie looked down at his own legs, felt the pain in his back, and wondered if he would ever again be able to sprint with the power that Reed was running now. Then Goldie lifted his head and saw Reed break tape.

A new school record and the cheering stormed Goldie's ears. From now on Reed would have the cheers, the ribbons, the newspaper clippings. Goldie was no longer "King of the Quarter-Mile." And at that moment he hated that race with all his heart.

Your Turn

You can be loved by a friend in January and hated by that same friend in March.

You can be the most popular person in school, or on the job, one year, and the next year be forgotten.

Jesus was greeted with palm branches and shouts of praise as He rode into Jerusalem. He knew the cheering of the crowd. But a few days later that same crowd nailed Jesus to a cross.

"I have suffered the loss of all things, and do count them but dung, that I may win Christ" (Phil. 3:8, KJV).

1. What have you lost in your life that is valuable to you?
2. Did you appreciate this "thing of value" more when you had it, or after you lost it?
3. What did losing a "thing of value" teach you about appreciating it?
4. In time, do we have to give up God's gifts that are important to us?
5. How can you appreciate a blessing in your life today that you may not have tomorrow?

22

The Boredom Factor

He ran. He hopped. And then he skipped down that runway. Soon he was leaping into the air, landing with his feet in front of him, splashing sand, and at last diving forward with his whole body.

The event is called the triple jump, which is a more adult term for the "running hop, skip, and jump."

Pete was Wykoff's best triple jumper. He was an exceptional athlete who loved sports.

His father did not love sports.

But whenever Pete played basketball, his father was there. Shorter than his son, he would sit with an overcoat and a fur hat, munching on popcorn. Pete's father was bored by the game; everybody ran around too fast. But when Pete would go in for a lay-up, or make a brilliant shot, Father would drop his bag of popcorn, clap his hands and swell with pride.

It meant a great deal to Pete to have his father at the game, even when he looked bored.

One more jump and Pete would win the triple jump. He bent over. Then he straightened his body. Suddenly he fired down the runway, carefully pacing each step.

Then the hop. The skip. The jump . . .

. . . *High into the air. Glide to earth . . .*

. . . His feet rammed into the pit and sand splashed out. He plunged forward, landing on his hands and knees—the champion!

The crowd cheered and gathered around him, patting him on the back.

Then, in the back of the crowd, I could see a man in an overcoat and fur hat, considerably smaller than the athletes surrounding him. This man began to elbow his way through the crowd, pushing past runners and coaches. Reaching the center of the crowd, he gently put his arms around the champion.

"I'm proud of you, Son."

"Thanks, Dad."

"You were marvelous!"

"I was nervous with all these people watching."

"I don't know much about track," his father said, "but sometimes when I'm bowling, and the rest of my team expects me to get a good frame, why, I get nervous too."

Father rubbed Pete's back with his hand, and the champion moved close to him. Pete's face said, "This is my father. I love him."

"Pete?"

"Yeah."

"Now that you've won, do you want to go home? All this track business is boring me to death."

"Aw, Dad," he laughed.

"I love you, Son," his father whispered softly.

Your Turn

There are many good things you neglect to do for God, or for other people, because these things go against your line of interests. To put it bluntly, they bore you.

You don't feel studious, so you don't study the Word. You consider yourself an action type person, so you don't pray. You're shy, so you don't witness about Christ. There are a thousand excuses you can make for not bringing joy to the heart of God.

Ask the Spirit to give you a new attitude toward "unpleasant" Christian labors. Along with your prayer, think about this verse and what it means, "The joy of the Lord is your strength" (Neh. 8:10, KJV). May the strength of Christ help you endure even "boredom" as you follow the risen Savior.

"I can do all things through Christ which strengtheneth me" (Phil. 4:13, KJV).

1. Have you ever been proud of your parents? A guardian? A brother or sister? Have these people ever been proud of you?
2. What positive lessons did you learn when you made someone else proud of you?
3. Which tasks in your Christian life bore you?
4. What do you plan to do about this boredom?
5. Is there a certain task that you don't want to do even though such a task would make another person happy?
6. What can be done today to help you joyfully do all things for the glory of God?

23

When Your Enemy Is Hurting

The crowded bus was unusually quiet, even though it was packed with both guys and girls. They were silent because today would be the last meet of the season.

The runners tightened and retightened their spikes with their little wrenches. Occasionally someone would call out, "Hey, Rowdy!" above the rumble of the bus, and our easy-going student manager would send a roll of tape toward the back of the bus. Hopefully it would get to the right person after passing through a dozen pairs of hands. But despite these actions, there was still a strange silence. Many minds were grinding and churning as the bus rolled along.

I too was thinking.

I thought of Rick. He had graduated last year, but not as a conference pole-vault champion. I prayed that he had learned something about the victory of defeat. And I hoped that today, somehow, I could teach this team what I thought Rick had learned. For there was a great possibility that many of these athletes would face defeat today. Jamie would be sprinting on a pulled muscle. Goldie would be racing in the hated 400 for perhaps the last time, though he had hardly raced all year. Sherri, with courage, would be running again. How would Sam do? Pete? Reed? Don? Lynn?

"This is the district track meet," I said, standing and gripping the bar tightly so that I would not fall over. "If you can finish in one of the first three places in your event, you'll go on to represent Wykoff in regional competition. If you don't place in the top three, well, then this is your last meet of the season. If you're a senior, I don't need to say more."

I looked at Jamie. Goldie. Wendy.

"Sure we're a small team," I said. "But stand strong. Don't be afraid. *Fight.* Fight against the big schools. Don't let them push you around."

I knew that my teams needed every resource available as they went into this meet. So I was giving the impression that the other schools in the district were our bitter enemies, that they loved ridiculing Wykoff because we were small. I was trying to get my team angry; I was trying to create an enemy. I wanted the force of that anger to be translated into physical power, worked out in running, vaulting, leaping, and throwing.

Our bus pulled into the large parking lot. I could see the modern school building and Elgin-Millville's all-weather track.

One of the buses of our "enemies" pulled alongside of us. And we all watched Spring Valley's coaches and athletes step off that bus. Now I think very highly of that town, but upon entering competition today, Wykoff and Spring Valley would be mortal enemies. One team would be the conqueror, the other the defeated. But she did not look like an enemy as she got off the bus.

Glenda gave our bus a friendly, pretty smile. A smile that said: "I like you. I hope you do well today." Carrying her spikes in one hand and her starting blocks in the other, she walked toward the school building.

Glenda was perhaps one of the greatest athletes that Spring Valley had ever seen. Today she was expected to take at least three firsts. Many thought she would break the Minnesota record in the 100-meter low hurdles at the state track meet. But I was to coach against her. As soon as the first starting pistol was fired, she too would become my enemy.

"Make sure you warm up," I said to the team as I stepped off the bus, clutching my clipboard tightly. I had to go into the school building for a "scratch meeting" with the other coaches.

Everyone was pleasant in the meeting, but when these coaches stepped into the sunlight and onto the field, they would all become enemies to each other.

The meeting ended and crowds milled around as I pushed my way out of the school. The meet had already started.

Gun shot!

The 100-meter low hurdles had begun. This was Lynn's race.

Too bad I couldn't talk to her more before she ran, I thought, *and boost up her spirit.* But it was too late now.

Gun shot!

My heart stopped with the heart of every coach who had an athlete in this race. A second gun shot immediately after the first means that all the runners are called back to the starting blocks because someone has jumped the gun. And the runner jumping the gun is disqualified from that race.

Disqualified—weeks, months, and even years of dreams and training cast away into a cruel wind. Jumping the gun at this meet would keep a runner from going to state.

Was it Lynn? Did Lynn jump the gun? I couldn't see from where I stood so I shoved through the crowd for a better look. Lynn would be in tears and I would try to comfort her.

Through the wire mesh fence I could see a girl lying facedown on the pavement in front of the starting blocks. *Lynn?*

No. It was Glenda from Spring Valley. My fingers gripped the mesh and my face was tight against the fence. I could see Glenda, but I had not seen what had happened. Yet I could imagine it in my mind.

The starter had called out the cadence.

"Runners to your marks!" and the hurdlers flexed their leg muscles and positioned their starting blocks.

"Set!" The last word before the gun. Glenda's fingers were arched. Those small fingers had to support the entire body. The gun was destined to go off one second after the calling of "set." But it seemed so much longer than a second.

How much longer is this starter going to take before he pulls the trigger?

Glenda was eager to explode out of those blocks and win the race. The crowd expected it. Her coach expected it. And Glenda, in her humble way, expected it. But how long could fingertips hold her up?

Then, in that eternity, her fingertips gave away—not much, but enough. Her body flinched forward only a nudge before the gun shot. But it was enough for the starter to pull the trigger again.

An accusing finger pointed at Glenda. "It was *you.*"

Shattered dreams.

Glenda, in tears, had toppled to the pavement, a vicious end for her high school track career. Her nose struck the solid all-weather track, and blood streamed out, blood mixed with tears. And my soul screamed inside me.

I gripped the mesh fence even tighter. One of her coaches cradled Glenda in his arms and headed for the bus. The same bus that she had stepped out of earlier with a warm, loving smile for her "enemies."

Was Glenda an *enemy*? Her dreams had been shattered in the same way that any Wykoff person's dreams could be shattered. She cried the same tears my young men and women cried.

No. She was not an enemy made of paper, pasted on the pages of opposing record books. She was a person, created in God's image.

How, at that moment, I wished that Glenda could get back in the blocks. When that gun sounded, all of us, including Lynn, would have yelled ourselves hoarse for Glenda to cross the finish line a victor.

But all this, too, was a shattered dream.

I had died to being an enemy.

With my face still against the fence, I wanted to shout a word of comfort, a word of healing, a word of encouragement to Glenda, my enemy. But the crowd swallowed her up, and I could see her no more.

Your Turn

We all have enemies. But God protects us from them. And Christ died for even our worst.

Ask God to teach you how to love your enemies. Don't condone the sin of your enemy, or fall into that same sin. Don't preach against the sin of your enemy unless you have first confessed that sin in your own life. And above all, let God show you that there are many people your imagination calls "enemy" who are really your friends.

"Love your enemies" (Matt. 5:44, KJV).

1. Do you ever enjoy calling another person "enemy"?

2. Do you change your opinion of someone if you find out that he or she is a member of another political party? From another country? Another race?
3. Christ asked us to love those whom our heart calls enemies. Can someone still be your enemy if you love that person?
4. How can you love a person without falling into his sin?
5. Can you love a Communist? A Nazi? A Satan worshiper?
6. Who have you wrongly looked upon as your enemy? Can you change that outlook both today and tomorrow?

24

Learning from Others' Mistakes

Mike's powerful legs reminded me of oak trees. Those legs would burn up the track in either the 100 or the 400. They could just about fly in the long jump or sail high into the air over a bar. He was a tough competitor, and he had dreams of being a champion.

At most meets he brought the team valuable points. But today was District Saturday, and the competition was fierce. Mike would not grab any first places. In fact, I doubted that he would even place. But Mike was priceless to our team.

He was the spark plug. He would encourage or rebuke, whichever the team needed. Mike was a team man. No, Mike would not be a champion today, but his defeat would inspire him to help others become champions. He had learned how to mine jewels from loss. Today he had failed at district, so he would show others how not to fail.

I stopped him as he walked away from the high-jump pit and asked him how he was doing. He smiled and nodded his head. As always, he told me he was doing fine.

"We're sure coming out of this meet okay, aren't we?" Mike said.

"You bet," I said. "So far three district champions. I feel great."

Mike looked at the dirt and scraped his foot against the ground. The wind tousled his hair. "Funny how Glenda helped us," he said.

I thought a moment. "Yeah. That's true. Glenda helped us a lot."

"Maybe Sam would've been the one to jump the gun if Glenda hadn't."

"Or Pete or Wendy or Lynn . . ."

"Too bad it had to happen," Mike said. "But we all learned from it."

I tapped my clipboard against my leg a few times and thought out loud, "Glenda had a dream of winning hurdles at state. She didn't sacrifice winning that event on purpose, but she still sacrificed. Because of her sacrifice, everybody has been more cautious about their starts. Because of Glenda's tragedy, we haven't had one tragedy on our team today. We owe a lot to Glenda . . ."

Gun shot! Both of our heads whipped toward the gun as the girls took off in the 200-meter low hurdles. A new race for girls in Minnesota, it was half a lap of low hurdles. The effort of sprinting 200 meters with the added effort of striding over hurdles made it a grueling race. At the conclusion of the race, the runners were often so tired that form became pathetic. When form is bad, it's easy for the runner to stumble over the hurdles.

Glenda was out in front. I had no girls in this final heat, so my eyes were on her. Her strong but petite legs glided forward with a smooth stride.

First hurdle. Her lead leg was out. Her opposite arm forward. Perfect. Glenda's powerful stride increased the gap between her and second place. Her arms kept pumping. Second hurdle, perfect. Stride. Stride. Stride. Hurdle? Perfect.

Halfway and she was still in first place. Would she win this time? No one else was even near her. Would she keep that form? That speed? Or would she exhaust herself, trip up, and—

I hated the thought.

I dropped my clipboard and cupped my hands around my mouth. "C'mon, Glenda!" I yelled.

Mike's eyes left the race and gave me a puzzled look.

You should understand, Mike, I thought. *You lost today, but you transformed your defeat into victory by helping your teammates. Your dreams died so that others' dreams could live. Everybody at this track meet has been helped by the death of Glenda's dream, but that doesn't mean that another of her dreams can't live. If others have learned from her failure, can't she learn too?*

Love your enemies.

Suddenly his hands shot up. "C'mon, Glenda!" he screamed.

Stride. Stride. Stride. Hurdle? Perfect.

Then I could see her face. Each pump of the arm took her further away from her lost dream.

Her eyes saw new dreams and unexpected goals. *Look up. Head up. The tape is near. Ahead!*

She broke the tape.

Glenda, our former enemy from Spring Valley, was now the district champion and record holder. In two weeks she would be the state champion and the new state record holder.

Your Turn

Sin is ugly and horrible. Sin *kills*.

God tells us in the Bible about "super" Christians who have sinned: Moses, Aaron, David, Peter. May you learn from their mistakes so that you don't make those mistakes. May you be sensitive to the mistakes that other people make so that you don't make the same mistakes.

Ask God to forgive your sins because of Jesus. Let go of the bitterness and the guilt you feel for your mistakes. Leave broken dreams behind you and run forward into new dreams. Ask God to use your mistakes as teaching examples for other people so they won't fall into sin.

"But with many of them God was not well pleased: for they were overthrown in the wilderness. Now these were our examples, to the intent we should not lust after evil things, as they also lusted" (1 Cor. 10:5-6, KJV).

1. Can you think of a time when a teacher or someone else used your mistakes as an example for "how a person should not act"? How did you feel?
2. When you read or see another make a mistake, do you learn from that mistake?
3. Ask your parents or some other person you trust to tell you the one mistake they made in their life that they pray you won't make.

4. Think of another person who is in danger of making a mistake that you have made. Would it help to talk to that person?
5. Do you dwell on your mistakes? Do you forget them? Do you ask God to forgive them?
6. What can you do tomorrow to help you learn from your mistakes and from the mistakes of others?

25

Troublemaker vs. Champion

When he was only in the seventh grade he ran the varsity 800-meter race. Now, 800 meters is a long journey for a seventh grader, but he was told he had talent as a distance runner. So by the time he moved into senior high, he was very effective in this event. However, when I took over the coaching spot, he convinced me that he should be a sprinter.

So we worked at making him a champion sprinter. He pictured himself as district champion and always kept that vision before him. He wasn't a champion yet, but his vision never wavered.

What did others say about his goal?

"Well, Reed, you might look like a sprinter, but you've got a long ways to go," an opposing runner told him.

"How come Reed's in the 200 today?" Wendell, a teammate, would ask me. "He's no sprinter; he's a distance man."

Reed's parents were kind and encouraging. But even they had their healthy skepticism. "Reed, are you sure you want to be a sprinter? You did so well in the 800." But then Reed's dad would confide in me with a laugh, "The crazy kid can do anything he puts his mind to."

Many people questioned me about making Reed a sprinter. But Reed never doubted my judgment.

I must confess I too was skeptical. Reed was improving constantly as a sprinter, but he had to train from scratch. He had been a good distance man and I could have built upon his strength, talent, and achievements. Perhaps he could still be an excellent 800 runner instead of just a good sprinter.

"I believe in you, Reed," I would say. God had permitted me to see great potential inside of Reed—more than just a sprinter.

Years before, somebody, somewhere, branded Reed as a "troublemaker." And even though these words were lies, they had come from a trusted adult. So to the small child Reed, these words were true. Under that curse, he felt an urge to create trouble. I saw a special person beneath these accusations—a person created in God's image. I wanted Reed to see this special person and not live under the label "troublemaker."

"I believe in you, Reed."

One year after Reed's switch from distance man to sprinter, he held the school record in the quarter-mile. And he had been burning up the 200 all season. But for the district meet, I put him in the lineup as my number one 100-meter-dash man.

"But he's not the best," some people argued.

"I hope you know what you're doing," complained others.

"Aw, he's a troublemaker."

"Reed, I believe in you," I told him, as we walked the halls together in school. "I know you can beat those other guys. I believe in you."

District Saturday came, and my stomach churned. I had witnessed Glenda's false start, and rejoiced when Sam took first place in the hurdle preliminaries. Now, the 100-meter dash. If Reed failed today, it would be a strategic failure on my part and would cost us a trophy.

"Runners to your mark!"

Something hammered inside me.

"Set. . . !"

I believe in you, Reed.

Gun shot! Sixteen feet mercilessly beat into that all-weather track. Spikes flashed. Faces strained in determination.

Reed leaned with his chest; he finished second. He was in the finals! I breathed out; I could relax. But the finals were staring into my gut all too soon.

The 100-meter dash—the crowning race for a sprinter. And Reed was in the finals!

I gripped my stop watch tightly. I looked into the face of Reed's mom, of Wendell. I stared at Reed.

Gun shot!

The mass of people shouted. The voice of Reed's father bellowed in my ears. I could see the row of eight young men stampeding toward me. Spikes pounding. Arms pumping.

But Reed could not see me. Instead, he saw a vision of what he was not. He saw a vision of district champion.

"Troublemaker!"

The roar of the crowd was silent in my mind. I could see Reed even with the leader.

"Troublemaker!"

Champion.

"Troublemaker!"

Champion.

I believe in you, Reed.

As I remember, it was all very quiet. All the runners had stopped; everyone had crossed the finish line. Reed was still in his lane, his arms pointing to the sky. He was the new district champion.

Reed marched through the crowd of people. And standing before me, he threw his arms around me.

Your Turn

People looked at Peter and saw an impetuous and frightened fisherman. Jesus looked at Peter and saw the leader who could feed His church.

Some people looked at Mary and saw an immature, unmarried, pregnant girl. God looked at Mary and saw the woman who would give birth to Jesus.

"But Ananias answered, 'Lord, I have heard from many about this man, how much evil he has done to thy saints.' . . . But the Lord said to him, 'Go, for he is a chosen instrument of mine' " (Acts 9:13, 15, RSV).

1. Think of the people who have called you bad names. Do you believe the names they have called you? Should you?
2. What have you told yourself, or what have other people told you that you cannot do? Is there any proof to these claims?
3. Other people's opinions of you can cause you to hate yourself.

Yet Jesus said that you should "love your neighbor as you love yourself." Do you find yourself lovable?

4. Do you believe that all your sins are forgiven because of Jesus? If your sins are forgiven, how does this make you feel about yourself?

5. What important things have you not done because of other people's opinions about you?

6. What can you prayerfully do tomorrow to improve your self-image?

26

Does Anybody Believe in Me?

It amazed me to see her short, pudgy legs shoot her to the bar and then send her sailing high into the sky, to tumble on the cushion below.

She popped to her feet and sprinted over to her coach. I tried to get her attention, but she didn't see me. As I walked away from the high-jump pit to talk to Reed before his race, I could hear her coach behind me. "Mattie, I believe in you."

The Mattie who had been declared ineligible and had moved out of town had made the track team of another school. On this District Saturday she was doing fantastic in the high jump. And she would go on to be the regional champion. Her coach believed in her.

One year later, Reed suffered a vicious motorcycle accident. Why does everything change so quickly?

St. Mary's Hospital, Rochester, Minnesota—one of the largest hospitals in the world, a hospital of tremendous prestige because of its connection with the Mayo Clinic. I stepped onto the curb, crossed the sidewalk, and walked up the stone steps to the front entrance.

Reed lay there alone in the sterile hospital room. He looked pale, but his eyes were bright and his smile told me he was going to make it. After our talk, I left the room confident that Reed was going to be all right. And my hunch held true. Reed did not grow up to be a "troublemaker." He recovered from his injury, worked hard, married, and set out on the path where he would follow Christ.

I crammed into the full elevator and we stopped at the fifth floor. The doors slid open and in walked a familiar face.

"Wendell!" I said, squeezing his hand. "How're you doing? Did you know that Reed's in—"

"Coach," he interrupted, deep concern creasing his face, "my sister Mattie's a patient here too. She's bad off. Maybe you could go talk to her."

As I walked the long hall to Mattie's room, I wrestled with many thoughts. *Maybe she doesn't want to see me. Maybe I'm a symbol of her old failure—her ineligibility. I hope she's all right.*

I stepped into the room. Her body was buried underneath blankets. All I could see was her somber, colorless face. She curled up her nose, squinted her eyes through her pop-bottle glasses, and at last recognized me.

"Hi, Coach," she said.

"Hi, Mattie. How're you doing?"

She winced, and then she smiled. "I don't mess with hard drugs," she answered me. "None of that. But I had been drinking beer. Then I just blacked out completely. I guess I went to the beach at Lake City, but I don't even remember that. One second I was in my car, the next I was up here in Rochester getting my stomach pumped. The doctors say that I'm allergic to alcohol. If I drink even a little, it might kill me."

I forced a smile. "That's a good reason to quit, isn't it?"

"Oh, the best. Never again. *Never again,*" she repeated.

But the words "it *might* kill me" ate right into my soul. "Might" was just too big a word.

"Mattie," I began, "you got shaken up quite bad, but you'll get over this with time. When you get over it, will you be tempted to take a drink?"

"No, I won't—"

"Just a minute, Mattie. Please let me finish. There's a national disease sweeping this whole country. It gets people to down or sniff or smoke or inject away all their problems. This disease doesn't want you just to throw away problems. It wants you to throw away your dreams, your goals, and your happiness. This disease is a liar and a sin. It can't take away anybody's problems.

"Drug abuse is everywhere and it's calling you to be a part of it by the smiling faces on a TV beer commercial, or in the laughter of friends chugging at a party. The world says you have to drink to really live, to have fun. Mattie, whether you like it or not, when you get out of this hospital, the world is going to put pressure on you to go back to drinking. Are you going to give in?"

Mattie's face was firm and determined. *"No, I'm not!"* she barked out.

But alcohol's deceitful call is a force that could defeat a thousand armies. It mocks common sense and self-preservation. It's an evil spirit that even the strongest of humans have trouble conquering.

There was a silence in that hospital room that did not want to end.

"Mattie," I said at last. "Just quitting drinking is not enough. God can forgive you because of Jesus. In fact, Jesus was punished on the cross for all your sins and mistakes. You *are* a region champion. Now, what just happened looks like a big defeat in your life. But God can also forgive you for your defeats. He wants to use your defeats to teach you valuable lessons. Today you have learned not to mess with alcohol because it will kill you.

"But now, ask Christ to guide your life. Make Him the most important person in your life. Serve God with your whole life. God wants to use you to build His kingdom. He needs you and He needs your clear mind. The Holy Spirit will help you live a righteous life. The Spirit of God will fight your battles, and you will win your war with the bottle."

Mattie nodded her head in agreement, and her face said she believed my words. She showed me her new Bible and told me about her recent prayer of dedication to Christ with the hospital chaplain.

I have seen many people turn to Christ at crisis periods in their lives. Sorry to say, when the bad times were over and the good times returned, Christ was forgotten with the bad times.

Will you be different, Mattie? What can I say to you? What can I say to you now to assure me that you will be different? That you will stay with Christ?

"Mattie?" I said. "God believes in you."

She never took another drink.

Your Turn

People can be champions in sports, business, politics, or entertainment, but lose their souls. Winning is good only if it puts your eyes on Christ. If winning makes you "bigger" and Christ "smaller," then you're better off losing.

God is great, and He calls you to do great things because He believes in you.

"Love . . . believes all things" (1 Cor. 13:7, RSV).

1. Think of the worst mistake you made in your life. What positive lessons did you learn from that mistake?
2. Do you turn to Christ only when times are bad?
3. Have you ever had to give up something to follow Christ? Is there something right now that you feel God is asking you to give up?
4. Have you ever heard someone say to you, "I believe in you"? How did these words make you feel?
5. God believes in you. How does that make you feel?
6. What can you do tomorrow to make your walk with Christ consistent in both the good and bad times?

27

If It's Not on TV, It Can't Be Great

It was District Saturday, but I found it hard to forget that cold day weeks before when Reed took his motorcycle test and Jamie pulled the muscle in his leg.

Jamie was the fastest man in the district. Every night he read the newspapers, comparing times of runners from other towns. He had a humble pride about his speed. He dreamed of being district champion in the 100-meter dash, but even more so in the 200. His dreams did not stop at district; they went on to regions and state.

Fortunately, the injury happened weeks before district. He missed the conference meet, but he would not miss the district. His pulled muscle kept hurting; it didn't want to heal.

I went to the district seeding meeting in La Crescent. I made Reed my number-one runner in the 100. But Jamie was my second man. He would also be running the 200.

"I can stride," Jamie told me in his soft Alabama voice. "I can shag and I can jog. I can pick up speed. But when I all-out sprint that's when I feel the pain."

"I don't want you to damage yourself," I said. "You're the best judge as to what you can do physically. But Jamie, is it the pain you're afraid of?"

He shook his head no. "Not the physical pain so much," he said. "I'm afraid that the muscle will pull out again if I open up in a sprint. I'm afraid that my leg'll go out. I don't want to go through that a second time because it could spell permanent damage. The pain, when I pulled it at Spring Valley, hurt something fierce."

We stood on the practice field together, fighting the hot sun and the strong wind. "Jamie," I said. "I think your leg is healed up enough for you to work on strengthening it. The district meet Saturday will be no picnic. There will be some fast boys there. And we've got a lot of hard work to do. I'm going to level with you. All this will be very tough. Do you want it?"

He looked into my face. The dream in his eyes was smoldering, but it was not in ashes yet. "I can do it," he said with a firm voice.

I made him run a slow mile and do stretching exercises. Then I made him run another slow mile.

"District!" I yelled. *District.*

Again, I made him stretch. *"Stretch."*

"Run a half mile at half your speed," I said. "Then run a quarter mile at half speed."

He walked up to me, hands on hips. The sun was making the sweat slide down his face. "Haven't run like this for a long time," he panted.

"Work. Hard work is the only route to go," I said.

Jamie smiled.

"Can you do it?" I asked.

"Sure, I can do it."

The infield of our track was a football field. I stood at one goal line, and Jamie stood at the other.

"Jamie!" I called out. "I want you to run to me at twenty-five percent of your speed."

He nodded and sprinted back to me. "Walk back to the other goal line and run it again at twenty-five percent," I said. He did. "How's your leg feeling?"

"You know it's funny," he said. "My leg's getting stronger. You must know what you're doing," he smiled.

"Run it again at twenty-five."

Soon he was running at fifty percent of his speed. Then fifty again. Fifty again. Again.

Then he was up to seventy-five percent of his speed. "You're doing great, Jamie," I said. "I'm proud of you. District."

Then he ran at seventy-five percent again.

"How's the leg feeling?" I asked.

"Good," he said. The courage in his face had grown stronger.

But it was not a courage in absence of fear. It was courage in spite of fear.

He raced at seventy-five percent again. Then again. Soon he sprinted at eighty percent. Eighty again.

"I'm feeling fine, Coach. I feel tired, but my leg's great."

"I'm proud of you," I said, as he walked back across the field. "I want you to run at ninety percent."

He looked at the ground, and bent over. All that we could hear was the roaring of the wind. Then he exploded into his run. Soon he was standing before me, fighting to catch his breath.

"Now ninety-five," I said.

For a split second, his face had a sickened look. Then he nodded his head and sprinted toward me.

"How're you feeling?"

"Tired," he said.

"Your leg?"

"Good."

"Walk back to the goal line," I said.

His leg's stronger and he knows it, I thought. *His confidence is strong. I've done everything I've wanted to do. But can he take it? Can his leg take an all-out sprint? If that leg goes out, so does his dream—and his confidence in me.*

"Jamie!" I shouted. "100 percent!"

"100?"

"Yes!"

For a moment there was a battle within him and it showed on his face. *I don't have to do this*, he thought. *I can walk away from all this. No one will blame me.*

The wind stopped blowing. The shot and discus throwers rested from their workouts to watch. The vaulters put down their poles. The long jumpers sat down so that they could see better. And the athletes who were through with their workouts eased out of the locker rooms. Everyone was silent. Everyone watched.

"Set!" I called.

Then I gave a shrill blast of the whistle. And Jamie was off. His start was fast, all out, building up speed.

"100 percent!" his teammates shouted.

I could see the fear in his face. He was like a man running on a frozen lake, at any moment the ice would break under him. But he ran on—full blast, with everything that he had, despite his fear of the muscle pulling.

Will the leg go? Will that muscle pull?

His spikes shredded the sod under his feet. *Did he feel the pain? Is the muscle going to pull?* He hit the seventy-five-yard line.

Jamie would set no records today, but this was his greatest moment as an athlete. He was racing against fear, and the stakes were high.

Jamie's legs were a blurred whirl. His face was strained with a deep exhaustion. His spikes dug into the grass with anger.

At last he crossed the goal line. He was bent over, gasping.

"How's your leg?" I asked, looking at his pain.

Jamie tried to catch his breath.

"How's your leg?"

He grasped both his legs; then he slowly straightened his body.

"How's your leg?" My whole being demanded an answer.

Jamie grinned, "My leg's all ready for Saturday."

His greatest accomplishment in all his years of sports happened on an ordinary weekday on the infield of a mud track in front of a crowd of everyday people. But those same everyday people saw a young man win a battle over fear that they would never forget.

Your Turn

God is always watching you—rejoicing when you come to Him and weeping when you turn away. Live every day with that thought in mind.

The greatest acts you can do for God often go unnoticed by the world. Acts of love are not done for publicity but for God and your neighbor.

The great accomplishment of your life will not be done before an audience. It will be done alone in prayer when you accept God's Great Accomplishment, Jesus Christ, as your Savior and your Life.

"Take heed that ye do not your alms before men, to be seen of them: otherwise ye have no reward of your Father which is in heaven" (Matt. 6:1, KJV).

1. You are watched by God all the time. How does this make you feel?

2. Do you have to receive recognition for a good deed before you will do that good deed?

3. Are you kind to people only when it will benefit you?

4. Are there certain jobs you feel God is calling you to do that you won't do because those jobs are not glamorous?

5. Do you believe that nuclear destruction and other catastrophes have been diverted by humble, anonymous praying people?

6. What are some unglamorous and thankless tasks you can do for God today?

28

Only a Friend Can Call You a Fish

I looked at Pete as the most important person on the team. His favorite saying was, "No guts, no glory!" He never missed a practice, and he gave us many points every meet. Pete gave 100 percent *all* the time and he encouraged his teammates to give that same 100 percent.

Goldie was his good friend, but Pete was disappointed in Goldie. He did not understand why Goldie wasn't having a better season or why Goldie no longer had the school record in the 400. But Goldie was not one to tell about his pain, so I didn't think that Pete fully understood Goldie's kidney problems. Goldie accepted the criticism from Pete, and even welcomed it. That criticism showed that their friendship was strong.

District Saturday.

I had many fears. Reed was my number-one man in the 100. And I had taken rebuke for that strategic move. And in that same race, an injured Jamie would be sprinting full force.

I made Jamie stretch and stretch and stretch again. I prayed that when the gun went off his leg would not go out.

Pete was our third man to be running in the finals. Pete would give 100 percent, as would Reed and Jamie. Goldie would see Pete give 100 percent and feel proud to be his friend.

The gun!

"Please, God," I prayed, "don't let Jamie's leg go out."

Reed was the winner. Pete placed sixth. And Jamie—fifth. Jamie stared at the ground.

"You didn't get to be champion," I said. "But you did your

best. A few days ago you were limping, today you're the fifth fastest man in the district. And you gave Wykoff needed points. I'm proud of you. But it's all behind you now. You still have the 200. You made the finals. Go get 'em."

Pete placed a hand on Jamie's shoulder. "Good race, Friend." Then he walked away. Pete needed to speak to Goldie before the 400.

Pete had been close by, days before, and had heard me talk to his friend. "Goldie, I want you to get back your school record. You've been out all season and the competition will be unbelievable at district. You're going to have to work hard today to make up what you missed. In fact, I'm going to work you into the ground. Harder than I worked Jamie."

Goldie's face was grim, but he nodded in agreement with what needed to be done.

That night at practice, Pete watched Goldie run the 400 at slow speed, medium speed, and in a sprint. He saw Goldie with a red face and a heaving chest. He saw Goldie with spit dripping down his chin and with an aching side. Pete understood the agony Goldie fought against.

But when Goldie staggered into the locker room, Pete was waiting for him. "Goldie, you're a fish," Pete said. "Fish" was a word he used for people who weren't giving 100 percent.

The district 400-meter race. The quarter-mile that Goldie so hated, but the race he wanted to win with all his heart. He was a senior and he wanted to hold the school record once more. His muscles were taut, waiting for the gun.

Pete's face was against the mesh fence, a stop watch hanging from his neck and clutched in his hand. If it weren't for the cold silence, he would be calling out to Goldie harsh words of encouragement.

"Set!"

Gun!

Goldie's face lunged at desire with the cheering loud in his ears. He quickened the pace going into the first curve.

Maybe the last time. Give it everything. Everything!

He could see Pete's face and he could hear his voice: "Goldie! You fish!" Goldie broke around the second curve into the straightaway.

Pete's blue eyes flashed. He shouted for his friend. He

screamed at Goldie. And as I looked into his face, I knew that Pete would have liked to have jumped into Goldie's body and given him his muscles, his legs, his lungs, and taken his pain if that would have helped Goldie to be the district champion and school record-holder.

Pete was running along the fence, his face tight with affection, rasping words shot out of his throat, "Goldie! You fish!"

Goldie, you have guts, Pete thought. *I wish I could give you my guts too. And we could add your guts and my guts together to beat all those weeks you couldn't work out. I'd give you my guts so you could have the glory.*

Then Goldie went into the last curve. The "brick wall." Agony smashed into him. His dry throat ripped open. His side caved in. His eyes popped out.

School record. Got to see my name in that trophy case once more.

Goldie's arms felt like he was carrying barbells. His legs took all his concentration just to keep moving. And then, the other runners began to pass him one by one. But Pete's spirit stormed and howled in his heart: "Goldie! You fish!"

Goldie staggered out of the last curve. The pain was choking him. Then he saw Pete at the finish line, his face tight against the fence. Goldie's legs pounded into the ground like sledge hammers. The cheers of the past and the present swallowed him up and he unlocked a forgotten reserve of power.

Goldie ran the last few meters giving his all, his guts, his 100 percent. He leaned and crossed the finish line looking every bit the champion.

He placed fifth, giving Wykoff points in the face of brutal competition. But he did not win back the school record in the 400 and he never would.

Pete clapped his hand on Goldie's back. "Great race," he said.

Your Turn

You may know Christ as a character in the Bible, as a word sung on a Sunday, or as someone you study. But do you really know Christ as a friend?

Christ is a real person and He wants to be your best friend. He gave His very life for you so that you could know the glory of God forever.

"No longer do I call you servants, for the servant does not know what his master is doing; but I have called you friends, for all that I have heard from my Father I have made known to you" (John 15:15, RSV).

1. Do your friends remain your friends after you make a mistake?
2. Do you stay friends with someone after he fails you?
3. How does it feel knowing that Jesus Christ wants to be your friend?
4. How does Jesus respond to you when you disappoint Him?
5. Pete wanted to give himself to Goldie for Goldie's sake. Jesus gave His life for you. How does this make you feel?
6. What can you do now to know Jesus as your best friend?

29

Behind Every Winner There's a Loser

Everything seemed to point in Lynn's favor. She had run excellent times all season. Her health was terrific, and her talent had continually improved as a result of hard work. Yes, she *would* go on to regions in the hurdles. But maybe I was getting too far ahead of myself. This was District Saturday. Lynn had not run yet. Before she could go on to regions, she would have to place at least third in the 100-meter low hurdles.

I talked to Lynn before she headed toward the starting blocks for the final heat. But then I had to find the meet master; there was a pressing problem concerning a pole-vault rule that I had to discuss with him. If I hurried I could be back in time for Lynn's race.

I walked into the school, and was soon outside again, pacing across the parking lot toward the track. I heard the crack of the starting pistol for Lynn's race.

Immediately, the starting pistol fired again.

No! False start! How could anyone false start?

I ran toward the track, bolting through the mesh-fence gate. I bumped into Pete, his eyes flashing in anger.

"Lynn's been disqualified," he said frantically. "You've got to talk to the starter. That was *no* false start. I was close by. The hammer of that gun came down but there was a delay in the shot. Lynn jumped when the hammer came down, before the gun made a noise. There's no way she should be disqualified."

"I'll see what I can do," I said grimly. I tucked the clipboard under my arm and walked to the starting line. The starter, with gun in hand, was involved in an intense discussion with a meet official. Lynn was behind the blocks, trying to untie her spikes. Suddenly, her whole body broke into a sob.

"Stupid one-start rule," I muttered between clenched teeth and then stepped up to the platform. I looked into the starter's face, "Excuse me, sir. I'm on the games committee and I challenge your disqualification of my hurdler—"

But then I realized that the starter's attention was not directed toward me at all but rather to a girl on his left in a black uniform. The uniform was from Spring Valley. I recognized the girl as Penny, and another Spring Valley hurdler was standing next to her.

"Yes, sir," Penny said to the starter, "I heard it. The gun clicked before it went off. You may not have heard it, but I did. I want to remind you, sir, that you can't call a false start on a click." She spoke in a voice that was firm and respectful.

The starter looked at the other official. The official shrugged his shoulders. If the starter could change his decision without feeling too foolish, then maybe everything would be all right.

"Because the ruling has been challenged," the starter said, waving his pistol as he talked, "and because of the confession of the opposing runner, I cancel the disqualification. Wykoff, return to your lane."

Penny let out a whoop. The other Spring Valley hurdler clapped her hands together in joy. Both girls ran over to Lynn, and all three hugged one another.

Lynn climbed into the blocks for a second time. The pistol fired. And there was no false start. Lynn ran like a bullet, excited and thankful to be back in the race.

Hurdle after hurdle Lynn hit with good form, gliding gracefully over each one. Lynn finished third. Penny fourth. Lynn was on her way to regions. Penny was not. And only Penny knew that the race would turn out this way.

Your Turn

God is self-giving love. He sacrificed His only Son for our benefit.

If Christ lives inside you, expect Him to manifest His life

through you in sacrificing for others in a self-giving love.

"Present your bodies as a living sacrifice, holy and acceptable to God, which is your spiritual worship" (Rom. 12:1, RSV).

1. Think of a sacrifice someone has made for you. How did it make you feel?
2. Have you ever made a sacrifice like the sacrifice Penny made for Lynn? If not, why haven't you?
3. What would you have done if you were Penny?
4. What has God sacrificed for you?
5. Is sacrifice ever a bad thing?
6. Can you make a complete sacrifice of yourself to God today?

30

Fifth-Place Victory

The district 200—Jamie's race. It was his final hope for championship, his very last shot at a dream. For two years I had listened to him talk passionately about the 200, reciting his times to show that he was improving in each race. He was certain in his own mind that he could beat the other runners in the district, and he couldn't wait for the day to prove it. All this was said before the cold day when he pulled his leg muscle. An injury can change so many things.

So Jamie waited for the 200. His hope. His dream. He no longer was afraid of his leg going out. Now he feared that he might not win.

The gray whisp of smoke popped up out of the gun, and I pushed down my stop watch. Eight young men sprinted hard for 200 meters.

The race was over.

Jamie had his head down as he walked away from the awards platform. In one hand he carried his spikes; in the other, his fifth-place ribbon for the 200-meter dash.

"Jamie," I called from behind him, "you have nothing to be ashamed of." He stopped walking. He turned to me and tried to smile. "You showed courage," I said. "And you conquered obstacles that those other runners didn't have to face. If you didn't have the obstacles of pulled muscles and missed practices, you'd have a first-place medal in your hand right now."

Jamie turned away from me, "But, Coach, I *dreamed* of first place. I *wanted* first place."

"But you didn't get first place—" Suddenly there was a loud cheering. The boys' two-mile run had started. "You didn't get your dream," I said. "But you contributed to a larger dream. You aren't district champion, but Pete isn't either. And Goldie doesn't have a school record. But all three of you guys ran your absolute best. And all of you guys have given your team valuable, *valuable* points.

"Don't be ashamed of yourself. This is a close meet. If we win a trophy today, it will be by just a few points. The points Pete and Goldie and you earned."

I looked deep into Jamie's face as he gripped his spikes and his ribbon. His eyes were wet. Then he walked up to the track, peered into the mass of two-mile runners, and began cheering for his teammates.

Your Turn

You may never be as famous as Billy Graham, Oral Roberts, or Pat Robertson. You may never win a Nobel Peace Prize as Mother Teresa did. You may never become the pastor of a church or a church council president.

But you can help finish the job that all these other people have started. You can obediently carry out seemingly insignificant tasks of compassion toward others and witness to what Christ has done in your life. God may use this "fifth-place" action on your part to bring another one of His children home to the Kingdom of God so that person may receive the trophy of eternal life.

"On the contrary, the parts of the body which seem to be weaker are indispensable" (1 Cor. 12:22, RSV).

1. Can you think of a time when your loss helped somebody else?
2. Sometimes we look at well-known Christians as "First-Place Christians" and ourselves as "Fifth-Place Christians." List the specific ways that God can use you and no other in doing His work.
3. God can use your losses to build up His kingdom. What does that mean to you?

4. Do you follow Christ because you want to win some crown or trophy on judgment day? Or do you follow Christ because He is Lord?
5. Has Jamie's story helped you look at a loss in your life as a victory?
6. What can you do tomorrow to share Christ with another?

31

There's Not Always a Next Year

The crowd was cheering in the distance. Cheering for Goldie, for Reed, for Jamie, for Pete. But there was no cheering where Don stood—in fact, there was not much of a crowd. The few fans watched in silence, an atmosphere vital to a man throwing the discus.

The discus is a disk of substantial weight. You let it rest in your hand and hook your fingers over the edge of it. Discus throwers usually throw the discus out of a spin while staying within the throwing circle. If the discus thrower does everything right, the discus will glide like a pie tin in the air. If the thrower does something wrong, the discus will wobble like a wounded bird falling to the earth.

At a track meet, the discus event usually starts before the running events, before the crowd arrives. Many times the discus throwers have to compete with no audience watching them. And in practice sessions, discus athletes work out apart from the rest of the team.

Don was a huge young man. His combination of strength, quickness and grace made him my number-one shot and discus competitor. He was not a glory seeker but a team man.

When Don stepped into the circle, spun around and released the discus, eyes would marvel at his grace and balance. Then those same eyes would follow the disk as it sailed through the blue sky and crashed to the ground.

Don threw the discus meet after meet, pulling more than his share of first and second places. But few teammates were there to cheer him on because most of those teammates were running. Few students from the school could make it to see him throw because the time for the event was so odd. I always tried to watch him, but I was often saddled with meetings. In short, Don had to compete without the cheers of his teammates or his friends. After the competition was over, he would board the bus alone. *Alone.*

One day he became District Champion.

Everybody said to him, "Oh, this is *the* year, Don. This is the year that you'll go to state." Colleges were interested in him. "This is the year." He went on to regions. "This is the year, Don."

His discus climbed into the sky like a satellite searching for an unknown planet and crashed a long way from where he stood. A second or a first place in regions would send him on to state. But Don did not go to state that year.

"Next year. Next year will be the year you go to state," they said to him. "Next year" was a refreshing vision of renewed hope.

"Next year" *did* come. He began practicing as soon as football season was over. He decided not to go out for basketball despite the urging of his coach, because he wanted to prepare for track. College coaches wrote him letters, wanting him for their track program. Then spring came.

Don was better than ever—quicker, more graceful, more powerful. He broke the school records, set twenty years before, both in the shot and in the discus.

"This is the year you'll go to state, Don, your senior year."

He placed high in the district. He would be competing at regions again, another shot at state.

The crowd, as usual, was small. Don could hear the larger crowd cheer for Sam as he ran the hurdles, but Don's teammates had promised they would come over to see him throw as soon as they could. Now it was his turn to step into the circle and throw the discus. But where were his teammates? Again he would throw alone, without the encouragement of the team. But he could do it for himself and his team. He threw well and made the finals.

The finals. *This is it.* He squeezed the discus and breathed deeply. Don twirled his body and released the discus.

Against the flame of the sun, the discus was a bright flashing orb in the sky. It fell to earth—his last throw. The tape was brought in for the measurement and the small crowd watched with bated breath. I was silent. Would he make it? Mitch, Don's father, and Lynn, Don's sister, watched apprehensively. Anticipation was tight on Don's face.

The measurement? Six inches away from second place. Six inches away from the state track meet.

Six inches away. Six inches? How could I come so close and not go to state?

But breaking through the disappointment, a voice tried to speak. A voice deep within, of dawn, of hope. "Next year, Don; next year is the year you'll go to state."

As the wind fluffed Don's black hair, he heard the officials read the names of the first-, second-, and third-place winners. They read his name—but he was not going to state.

He had done his best. He had worked hard and dared to dream. No matter how bitter the disappointment, he would be brave.

Then with a sudden shock he was reminded that he was a senior. *This time, next year would not come.* And he had to face that realization *alone.*

Your Turn

God is always nearer to you than your next breath, close to you even in your most bitter disappointments. God is in your tomorrow, but you can find God only in "the now." Look to God now, and ask Him to touch you. Work for God now. Don't wait for tomorrow to serve Him. That day may never come for you.

"Do not boast about tomorrow, for you do not know what a day may bring forth" (Prov. 27:1, RSV).

1. Don had to do a difficult task without the support of other people. How does it make you feel to do something tough alone?
2. To whom do you go for support?
3. What disappointments in your life have made you say: "This time, next year will not come"?
4. Don knew the bitter irony of missing his dream by inches.

Have you "missed a dream by inches"?

5. Can you always count on "tomorrow" to make up for losing today?

6. How can you best use the present time for God's glory?

32

The Good Old Days Are Gone

A hot June day.

The gym was packed with people for graduation. Programs flopped back and forth fanning sweltering faces. It was a happy day. Young men and women were leaving behind an old life to gain a new life of triumphant dreams, hopes, and desires. Maybe.

It was also a sad day as I would be saying good-bye to seniors. I would never coach Goldie or Jamie or Wendy again. I watched my track people, in cap and gown, snatch diplomas, and walk quickly away from the track, the school, and the town. What would the future hold?

Wendy, Goldie, and Jamie stood in front of the school.

"Funny. Looks *bigger* than it did in seventh grade," Goldie remarked.

Jamie reached over and patted Goldie's stomach. "Funny," he drawled, "you look bigger than you looked in seventh grade, too. Let's go inside. It's been three years since we graduated. I want to see what it's like in there."

"Wait a minute," Wendy said. "Maybe we shouldn't go inside."

"Why not?" Goldie asked.

"We might be disturbing classes," she said. "Anyway, we remember it for what it was, pleasant memories. But it won't be like it was; it'll be different."

"Aw, c'mon, Wendy," Jamie said. "Don't be silly."

"Yeah," Goldie said. "Let's go inside. It'll be just like old times."

140

But all three were hesitant as they opened the heavy metal doors and stepped into the past. The same old slamming locker doors, the laughter of friends, and the hurried footsteps of instructors. But new teachers looked at Goldie and Jamie and Wendy as strangers. People who were only children before were now grown up. The trio saw familiar faces, yes, and even chatted with those faces, but the graduates and the students were in different worlds. Goldie, Jamie and Wendy no longer struggled with the fear of not passing math, or whether they would make the basketball team, or who was going to have a party this Friday. The conversations were very short. It wasn't the same; they had to get away.

Goldie and Jamie and Wendy escaped to the newer wing of the school. There, Jamie grabbed the handle to the door of the gym. Perhaps the three of them expected to see a volley ball or a basketball game of their past inside that gym. Perhaps they thought that they could travel into their graduation by walking into that gym.

The door opened, but the gym was dark and empty.

The three turned away from the darkness and then glared out the glass door to the football field. Jamie and Goldie and Wendy ached with a painful longing for brisk night air, the melody of a brass band, and the excitement of a Friday night football game. Soon they stood on the track, clay and mud under their feet.

"You know," Goldie said, "this isn't the greatest track, but I'm proud of it."

"Sure," Jamie said. "I am too. This track is a symbol. We graduated from a school that had the courage to put education first. Our town and our school are small, but they're excellent."

Wendy nodded, and then said, "This track's not fancy, but it's seen a lot of guts."

"Hey, Goldie," Jamie said. "Let's see you run the 400 like you used to."

"I hate that race," Goldie said. "And look how out-of-shape I am." But he had to run it. Something inside compelled him. With Jamie timing him on his wristwatch, Goldie's feet beat into that mud track.

I feel great, he thought. *I can run just like I used to.*

But after half a lap he had no wind. Another hundred meters

and he was walking—not because he could not finish. He was sad.

It's not like old times. Nothing stays the same.

He stopped walking; he wanted to remember his dreams and goals of the past. *Have I lost the past?*

He bent over and scooped up a handful of mud from the track. He looked at the mud in his hand. Then he squeezed his hand, believing for a moment that he could squeeze into himself his high school days and return to a simpler time with fewer troubles.

Go back to the joy. The teamwork. Yes, go back even to the broken dreams.

But the tighter he squeezed, the more mud fell to the ground until his hand was empty.

Your Turn

You must let go of the past. But God is waiting to help you win the future. The past that you long for is only satisfied in the "now" and in the "future" with Christ.

"Say not, 'Why were the former days better than these?' For it is not from wisdom that you ask this" (Eccles. 7:10, RSV).

1. Look back to high school or junior high or elementary school. Do you long for those days? Do they look better to you than the present?
2. Ask your parents or some other adult if the "good old days" were really that good.
3. What makes a person long for the past?
4. "The past that you long for is only satisfied in the 'now' and the 'future' with Christ." Do you feel that this statement is true?
5. Do you think about the past and the future so that you miss the opportunities found in the present?
6. What can you do tomorrow so as to not live in the past?

33

Lose the Battle, but . . .

He was tall, fast in speed, and excelled in coordination.

In March, I placed a hurdle in the hall of the school and said, "Now, Sam, learn these three tasks. Do all three as you go over the hurdle and you will have your form down. Put your strong leg forward. Stick the opposite arm to the lead leg out in front of you. And lean forward with your trunk. Lead leg. Opposite arm. Trunk . . ."

Sam was tall, fast, well coordinated and he learned very quickly. He soon had his form down as he glided over the hurdle in the carpeted hall of Wykoff High. When we had our first meet at Chatfield, he almost won on his first day of competition. Yes, Sam *almost* won.

But he would be defeated again and again throughout the season. From each loss he learned either how to come out of the blocks quicker or how to improve on form, how to speed up between hurdles or how to pace himself. Defeat after defeat he learned and remembered something valuable.

He scored high in the conference and in the district. But no first places. He even went to the regions, but up there they trounced him. After that first year of track, Sam's career could be summed up by saying, "Sam was super for a beginner, but he lost a lot of battles."

One year later—district. Sam was stretching out, his leg up on a hurdle. He was bending his trunk toward that leg, limbering up his body for the 110-high hurdles. Then, he straightened up, adjusted his glasses, and looked right at me. "There's something you didn't push on us on the bus ride over here," he said.

"What's that, Sam?" I asked.

A slow smile crept across his face. "Preston's in our district. They've produced a lot of state champions."

I nodded my head. "They also have the 'Coach of the Year,' " I said. "I've got enough worries, Sam. And so do you. Besides, many of Preston's best graduated last year. Just do *your* best."

On that day, Sam made the finals.

He was in the starting blocks, eager to explode forward—like a race horse anticipating the gate to open.

"Runners to your mark!"

Sam's mind scanned all his past second- and third-place finishes. He pieced together his defeats, and formed a picture of what he should *not* do in this race.

". . . Set. . . !"

His hips were raised, his fingertips balancing his entire body.

The shot! He dived out of the blocks and his feet beat into the track. The first hurdle was rushing toward him. He didn't think, he just acted. Lead leg. Opposite arm. The lean. Clear. Off a bit, but that wouldn't happen again. Stride. Stride. Stride. *Do it right this time.* Perfect.

There were at least four hurdlers in front of him. Sam sprinted for the next hurdle. *Perfect.* Step. Step. Step. Hurdle? *Perfect.* Step. *Pass one runner.* Step. *Pass another.* Hurdle? Perfect. Pass. Pass. Step. Perfect.

Sam was ahead of everyone. He blasted toward the last hurdle . . .

. . . *Perfect.*

As I watched Sam sail over that last hurdle, an old cliché came to mind. It may be timeworn and redundant, but still pregnant with truth: "You can lose the battle, but still win the war."

Sam shot across the finish line, the new district champion.

Your Turn

God calls us to fight a war against evil. As in all wars, we will lose some battles. But we will win the war, because the war has already been won in Christ. Let's learn from our battle losses.

"For whatever is born of God overcomes the world; and this is

the victory that overcomes the world, our faith" (1 John 5:4, RSV).

1. What battles do you feel you have lost as a Christian?
2. List the positive lessons you have learned from these losses?
3. Do you think God has won the war against evil?
4. How do you handle not being "first place" in something?
5. Read Eph. 6:13-18. List how you can be better equipped in your war with evil.
6. What positive lessons learned from "battle losses" can you apply to your life?

34

You Are Necessary

I didn't take only guys to the district track meet. My girls were doing great, too. In fact, some would be advancing on to regions. The last event was the 1600-meter (mile) relay. Four girls were about to run: Sherri, Bonnie, Marni, and Sandy.

"Do your best. And no matter what the outcome, I'll be proud of you," I said to them.

Sherri was ready at the starting line, the baton tight in her hand.

Gun shot!

A quarter mile. The distance that Goldie so detested. The distance every girl on the team hated. Sherri attacked her lap, eager to do her best. At the end of 100 meters she was leading.

I looked away from Sherri for a moment to see if the other girls in her relay team were ready. Then my eyes went back to Sherri. I couldn't believe it. She was limping—a pulled leg muscle.

I thought of the pain Jamie had wrestled with. He had rolled on the ground in agony. I thought how Sherri must be going through that same pain. I expected to see her rolling on the track, clutching her leg.

But she wasn't. She was *still running*, hobbling around the track. Girl after girl was passing her. But she gripped tight to the baton. She knew what she had to do. Hobbling wasn't good enough for her, so she picked up speed, and hit the "brick wall" with the added pain of a pulled muscle. She struggled around the last curve. I could see the look of fear and pain and reddened frustration through the tears on her face.

Sherri limped into the exchange zone and smacked the baton into Bonnie's hand. We were in last place. Sherri's pulled muscle was a tragedy. We were so far behind everyone else that I thought it was impossible for us to get points in this event. But I was proud that we were still in the race because Sherri had the guts not to give up.

Bonnie was a dynamo. Her feet tortured the track. In a fury close to a miracle, she was swallowing up the space between her and the pack. Then she was passing the girls who had passed Sherri. Soon Bonnie was in sixth place.

Then she hit the "brick wall" and was knocked back to seventh place. But she could see Marni waiting for her at the line. She could hear the frantic cheers. She kicked it in.

Sixth place as Bonnie slapped the stick to Marni and collapsed in someone's arms.

Marni. Her short legs pumped. She ran hard, but she did not pass. Then she was passed by another runner. She hit the "brick wall," but Marni maintained the position that Bonnie had achieved. In pained gasps she handed off to Sandy.

Sandy moved smoothly, like a well-oiled machine. Her slender body flew in a perfect sprinter's form. Sandy had style and grace, a joy to watch. Her devotion to excellence and her willingness to dedicate herself to hard work had converted into the power that was dazzling everyone at this moment. She soon passed one girl, then another. Sandy blasted through the "brick wall" and passed another girl.

Her hair flew back, her mouth hung open, and her feet dug into the track. She moved closer and closer to first place . . .

. . . We were all waiting for her at the finish line; we were *so* proud of her. And of Bonnie, Marni, and Sherri.

The relay team finished in fourth place. I'm sure that any other group of girls would have come in last.

Your Turn

We need the "Sherries" to pioneer. To do bold new deeds for God, even if it means pain, hardship, and persecution. We need the "Sherries" to start a work for God and to have the courage to keep that work alive.

We need the "Bonnies" who have the spirit and the drive to give vitality and power to what the "Sherries" have started. We need the "Bonnies" to soar above and ahead with a new speed, to startle the imagination, so that all can see how far, how fast, and how deep we really can go with Christ. To help us understand the eternal achievements we can achieve by working in partnership with God.

We need the "Marnies" to maintain and preserve the work of God done before them, the work of the "Sherries" and "Bonnies." To show others the great deeds of the past by maintaining the spirit and the vision of those who have run before them.

And we need the "Sandys" to boldly finish the mighty deeds that have been started by people of God. For if a work of God is not finished, then the world has lost out on many blessings.

God needs you, whether you are a starter, energizer, maintainer, or finisher.

"There are many parts, yet one body" (1 Cor. 12:20, RSV).

1. What new task can you start for God in your church?
2. What can you improve upon in your church that other people have started?
3. What task, started by others, can you help continue in your church so that task does not die out?
4. What project in your church can you finish?
5. How often do you ask God to use you?
6. What can you do tomorrow to work in cooperation with someone else?

35

Nonconformists

I watched Jamie and Goldie and Wendy graduate. I watched all three lose their high school days forever. And I watched them gain a tomorrow that would be an eternal today.

Bright-faced Kyle was the valedictorian. He stepped behind the lectern in his long blue robe and began his speech. The subject? Nonconformists.

Nonconformists? Losers in the eyes of the world. Hair-covered hermits shut away in cabins on distant mountains, emerging in spring to shout their anger at the world in the same voice as an Old Testament prophet. Right? Or some political radical? A punk rocker?

No. Kyle talked about Jamie.

Jamie? A nonconformist?

"But many people claim that nonconformists aren't liked by other people," Kyle said. "Well, I can't agree. Jamie's the captain of his football and basketball and track team. He's the president of the student council and the homecoming king. Pretty good for a nonconformist."

Yes, I thought, *Jamie IS a nonconformist.*

He goes against the grain of the world. He breaks the mold. He defies the system. He's got the guts to be different, to be a "peculiar person." He doesn't go to drinking parties. He doesn't believe everything that's told him. Others lash out with vengeance and cruelty; Jamie responds to everyone with love and kindness. He's honest and upright in everything he does. To Jamie, "Christian" means nothing less than a person who depends completely upon Christ for salvation and for life. A person who will follow the risen Christ wherever He leads.

Yes, I gave the word a long and a tough look and I agreed. Jamie was a nonconformist.

After the ceremony, I walked through the receiving line for all the graduates. The sun was pounding down upon me as I stood before Jamie.

His face unveiled a long smile. We shook hands and smiled. "Good-bye, Coach," he said.

Your Turn

God has called you to a life that the average person does not live. God calls you to be a nonconformist. Don't give in to the sins of the world. But there are times when you don't want to be God's peculiar person. Sometimes you want to be like everyone else.

Ask God to help you be the person that He wants you to be. And don't live in a religious conformity that is far away from God. Acting religious can be a dangerous trap for a Christian.

"But ye are a chosen generation, a royal priesthood, an holy nation, a peculiar people; that ye should shew forth the praises of him who hath called you out of darkness into his marvellous light" (1 Pet. 2:9, KJV).

1. Must a Christian be a nonconformist?
2. Do your friends ever talk you into doing something harmful that you don't want to do?
3. Why is peer pressure so strong?
4. What in society did Jesus conform to?
5. What can you do tomorrow to be God's "peculiar" person?

36

Winning Isn't Always First Place

The last event, the mile relay, was over.

For all practical purposes, this long-awaited and much-dreaded District Saturday was over. The battle against the large school, La Crescent, and the highly-rated powerhouse, Preston, was no more.

Pete stood beside me. As did Jamie and Goldie and Sam and Don and Reed and Lynn and Wendy and Sherri. Then the whole team walked over to stand beside me.

I was almost at the end of my second year of coaching. Two very tough and challenging years. I had my doubts about myself as coach. My trials in the district's smallest school, on a clay and mud track had all been worth it.

Pete smiled at me from under his light blue cap with wings protruding from it. Don smiled at me too. So did the rest of the team. In their smiles I could tell that they also felt it had been worth it. I thought of the young men who had graduated last year. I thought of Rick. I wished that all of them could be here. Then I looked into each face: Sandy, Marni, Mike, Janie; I was so proud to be the coach of this team.

We all stood before the empty bleachers. We looked up into the press box at the top of those bleachers, where the statisticians were tabulating the order of the finishing teams from top to bottom.

My stomach churned. We could not play the numbers game. La Crescent was too big a school. But maybe victory was still ours in another way.

The statistician began to announce the boys' teams from last place to first. He read off town after town, but I didn't hear Wykoff. I was hearing Lanesboro, Lewiston, Caledonia, and Rushford, but I still didn't hear Wykoff. Then I heard Spring Valley, *but* not Wykoff.

I didn't know there were so many teams in the district. The statisticians's voice droned on. *Maybe we're so small they're neglecting us all together.*

My whole team was tense, and we all grabbed each other's shoulders.

Would Wykoff be read next?

"Third place," echoed the loudspeaker.

Who would be third place? Would it be us? Us?

"The third-place finisher," the statistician repeated, ". . . *Preston.*"

There was a shriek in my ears. My team cheered with joy. They picked me up into the air. *We were the District Runner-Up!*

No, we could not beat La Crescent. We didn't have the size. We had to spread out our athletes until they were in a state of exhaustion. *But we'd won a trophy. A beautiful trophy. The first track trophy in the school's history. We had confronted the obstacles and we had gained the victory. We had won a glorious spot that we had fought for and are proud of.*

As they walked up to get their first-place trophy, La Crescent looked puzzled over our enthusiasm for a runner-up trophy.

But I hugged the trophy close to me. Every member of the team wanted to see it and hold it. The trophy symbolized a tremendous victory. This trophy, with all our obstacles and problems, was greater than a state championship. We had proved that "winning isn't always first place."

As we all walked back to the bus with a jubilant song of joy, I took Pete and Jamie and Goldie aside.

"We just barely beat Preston," I told them. First-place finishes by Reed and Sam and Don rocketed us to the top of the competition. But points you guys made that looked so insignificant to you put us over Preston and got us this trophy."

As I walked back to the bus, I whispered a prayer of thanks to my wonderful God.

Your Turn

I had studied and toiled and strained for this victory. But it was through prayer that I learned I could "do all things" through Christ. Through prayer I learned that God wanted to help me in all areas of my life, both large and small.

God wanted me to succeed. Prayer paved the way for myself and my team to do our best and capture our dreams. In prayer, God puts dreams inside of us, but we need to pray until our dreams come true in God's way.

My girls' team placed fourth in the district, and my boys were runner-up, an excellent achievement. But the glory did not stop there. We also fared well in regional competition. Sam and I were the first Wykoff athlete and coach ever to advance to state competition. One year later, at the end of the season, we were ranked as one of the top thirty teams in Minnesota in our class.

Prayer is the answer to all your needs. Christ is the fulfillment of all your hopes and dreams. Everything you could ever desire is found *in Christ*.

"Pray at all times in the Spirit, with all prayer and supplication" (Eph. 6:18, RSV).

1. What is your biggest problem in prayer?
2. Are there certain things that hinder answered prayer? Look at Ps. 66:18.
3. "In prayer, God puts dreams inside of us, but we need to pray until our dreams come true in God's way." Do you agree with this statement?
4. List times that God has answered your prayers.
5. Has God ever said no to you?
6. When can you set aside a specific time today for fifteen minutes of prayer? Can you do this every day?

37

Winners on the Sidelines

The District Runner-Up Trophy sparkled in the school's trophy case.

I saw a young man back from the Navy roaming the halls, and at last, standing before the trophy. This young man was no longer on crutches. He no longer walked with a limp, but I knew it was Kelly.

He squinted through the glass to read each name engraved on that trophy, straining his eyes, searching, perhaps in vain . . .

There it was. *His name.*

Kelly had not run in any meets the year we won the trophy, but he had gone out for track. He had been injured, but he was still a part of the team.

He could not run, so others ran in his place. And now he could see his face in the reflection of the trophy case. He was a *winner*.

Your Turn

I am a sinner. I cannot fulfill the complete law of God. But Jesus fulfilled that law for me by living a perfect life.

I deserved death for my sin. But the loving God did not want my death, so Jesus was punished for my sin, and died so that I could live.

I deserved hell because of sin. But Jesus announced to hell that my punishment had taken place when He was punished for me.

I did not have the power to give myself eternal life. Christ rose from death so that I could live forever.

And now, when weariness and despair grip me, and I have trouble running the race of life, Jesus runs for me, holds my head up to the heavens, where the reflection of God's face shines into mine.

"He himself bore our sins in his body on the tree, that we might die to sin and live to righteousness. By his wounds you have been healed" (1 Pet. 2:24, RSV).

1. Has anyone ever taken a punishment that you deserved? How did it make you feel?
2. Think of the fact that Jesus died for your sins. How does this make you feel?
3. Jesus can be your best friend and He'll help you run the race of life. How does this make you feel?
4. What "races" in life have you tried to run on your own without Christ's help?
5. How can sin injure a person?
6. Do you definitely believe that Christ is the only way that you can be saved from sin and death and have true life? Have you made Jesus the most important person in your life? If you haven't, ask Jesus to forgive you now and be the Lord of your whole life.